New Asian Emperors

This book is dedicated to our families
and in memory of

James B. Haley
(1916–1988)

Dr C. Venkatesan
(1924–1998)

&

Tan Thye Bee
(1914–1992)

New Asian Emperors

The Overseas Chinese, their strategies and competitive advantages

Dr George T. Haley, Associate Professor and Director, Programs in Marketing and International Business, University of New Haven, Connecticut

Dr Chin Tiong Tan, Distinguished Professor and Deputy Provost, Singapore Management University

and

Dr Usha C. V. Haley, Associate Professor of International Business, New Jersey Institute of Technology

OXFORD AUCKLAND BOSTON JOHANNESBURG MELBOURNE NEW DELHI

Butterworth-Heinemann
Linacre House, Jordan Hill, Oxford OX2 8DP
225 Wildwood Avenue, Woburn, MA 01801–2041
A division of Reed Educational and Professional Publishing Ltd

 A member of the Reed Elsevier plc group

First published 1998
Reprinted 1999

British Library Cataloguing in Publication Data
A catalogue record for this book is available from the British Library

ISBN 0 7506 4130 4

Composition by Avocet Typeset, Brill, Aylesbury, Bucks
Printed and bound by Biddles Ltd, Guildford and King's Lynn

Contents

Features

Endorsements

'Westerners have long assumed that there is one right way to organize and conduct large-scale business, on a foundation of rationality, individuality, and impersonality. This excellent treatise on the business philosophies and practices of the powerful Overseas Chinese cannot fail to open Western minds to whole new ways of business thinking.

This book is a must reading for any business that wants to succeed in Asia. The authors have presented a masterly picture of how business is done by the Overseas Chinese.

Finally, a book to help Western business leaders understand the business philosophies and practices of the Overseas Chinese. Many practices of multinationals need to be altered if they are to compete with, or work with, the Overseas Chinese'.

Philip Kotler
S.C. Johnson & Son Distinguished Professor of International Marketing, J.L Kellogg Graduate School of Management, Northwestern University

'This book is very timely as it examines in a serious but readable manner both the strengths and weaknesses of the Overseas Chinese business community, and provides a framework for understanding how this vibrant community will resurrect itself from the current crisis. Most books on the Overseas Chinese business community have veered between extremes: either gushing with adulation, or portraying them as a semi-conspiracy. This book takes a balanced and holistic view, and weaves in the ethical and cultural traits of the Overseas Chinese with their management practices'.

Ho Kwon-Ping
President, Wah Chang Group (Owner of Banyan Tree Resorts) & Chairman, Singapore Institute of Management

'In the new Asia, especially after the crisis, there will be more and more Overseas Chinese marketers. This book is very important for those who want to deal with them successfully in the true market-based global economy'.

Hermawan Kartajaya
President, Asia Pacific Marketing Federation

'The Overseas Chinese are among the most important groups of entrepreneurs in human history. Their contributions in the forthcoming economic reconstruction of much of East Asia will necessarily be immense. The New Asian Emperors provides a considered, highly readable and insightful analysis of why they are so critical to the future of the region and how their contributions are likely to be made. This book should be core reading for anyone doing business in Asia at this crucial time'.

Bruce W. Stening
Professor and Executive Director, Australia Asia Management Centre, The Australian National University

'The Overseas Chinese represent what is arguably one of the most important economic and financial groups in the world, whose actions in the Pacific Rim and in other parts of the world have had profound effects on economic development, financial stability and instability, and the evolution of a wide range of industries in a global economic context. They also represent what is often a controversial economic and political force in countries dominated by other ethnic groups. This book provides a thoroughly authoritative and balanced assessment of the Overseas Chinese in terms of their roots, the role of family structures, management practices, and approaches to dealing with Overseas Chinese business groups – which themselves will have to evolve rapidly in the years ahead if they are to succeed as true multinational enterprises'.

Ingo Walter
Charles Simon Professor of Applied Financial Economics, Sydney Homer Director of the NYU Salomon Center, and Professor of International Business, Economics and Finance, Stern School of Business, New York University & Swiss Bank Corporation Professor of International Management, INSEAD

About the authors

Dr George T. Haley is the Director of the Marketing and International Business Programs at the University of New Haven, Connecticut, USA. His research has been published in major academic journals, and he has presented it to audiences of managers, government officials and academics. He has taught Marketing and International Business at Baruch College (New York); Fordham University (New York); the Instituto Tecnológico y de Estudios Superiores de Monterrey (Monterrey, Mexico); the National University of Singapore (Singapore); Queensland University of Technology (Brisbane, Australia); Thammasat University (Bangkok, Thailand); and, DePaul University (Chicago). He has also taught in executive development programs in the USA, Australia, Mexico, Singapore and India. Prior to entering academia, he worked in the private sector and consults with several companies on international strategy and industrial marketing issues. He currently serves as Regional Editor, South and Southeast Asia, for the *Journal of Business and Industrial Marketing* (USA), and also serves on the Editorial Advisory and Review Boards of several other academic journals.

Dr Usha C. V. Haley is an Associate Professor of International Business and Strategy at the New Jersey Institute of Technology's School of Management. She is also a Research Associate in the Managing Business in Asia Program at the Australian National University in Canberra, Australia. She has taught International Business and Strategic Management at several major universities in the USA, Mexico, Singapore and Australia as well as in executive development programs around the world. Her research has been published in major academic journals and presented at international conferences. She also consults with major companies on issues of international strategy. She currently serves as Regional Editor (Asia Pacific) for two academic journals and on several editorial advisory boards.

Dr Chin Tiong Tan recently joined the new Singapore Management University as its Deputy Provost. Previously he was a Professor of Marketing and Director of Continuing Education at the National University of Singapore. Professor Tan sits on the boards of several companies and advises senior management on strategy and marketing. He is a popular speaker at executive programs and conferences around the world. Professor Tan is the co-author of Philip Kotler's *Marketing Management: An Asian Perspective*, and the co-author of several other books on marketing in Asia.

Acknowledgements

A book of this nature cannot be written with the interest of a day or the support of one person.

We owe special thanks to the thousands of executives on whom many of our ideas have been tested and refined. In particular, the following gave generously of their time, expertise and understandings of Overseas Chinese business operations and environments so that we could interpret and project them for this book: Goh Cheng Liang, founder of the Wuthelam Group and his son, Goh Hup Jin, Chairman of Nipsea Holdings; Stan Shih, founder and Chairman of Acer; Wee Cho Yaw, Chairman and CEO of the United Overseas Bank Group, and his son, Wee Ee Cheong, Deputy President of the United Overseas Bank Group.

This book would not have been possible without the support and faith of our publishers. In particular, Jonathan Glasspool of Reed Academic Publishing Asia (Singapore) supported this project from the start, became a friend over its course, and was always willing to listen and to provide suggestions even late on Friday evenings; and, Kathryn Grant and Caroline Struthers of Butterworth-Heineman (UK) showed remarkable forbearance and support, especially as the project hit delays.

I would like to thank the many elderly Chinese retirees who, when I was a child in Texas, babysat with me and told me wonderful stories of the homeland they left behind and the sages who so influenced their thoughts and lives.

Finally, we owe special thanks to our families for their tolerance and sacrifice of time. Usha and I have to thank our two little kittens: Comet Baby, for her constant advice and unstinting support, and Marmalade, who frequently stayed up with us through the night while we wrote the book in Chicago and Canberra. Both kittens loyally stood on fax-watch to inform us when faxes would come from Chin Tiong in Singapore!

Besides the above, we respectfully dedicate this book to the memory of two very special people who fueled our interest in Asia: my father, James B. Haley, whose love of history and philosophy has inspired me throughout my life; and, Usha's father, my father-in-law, Dr C. Venkatesan, who passed away during the writing of this book, and whose understanding of Asian business served as both guide and motivation.

George T. Haley
Chicago, May 1998

My father's Asian values of extraordinary hard work, controlled passion, learning, humility, devotion to his family and sense of duty inspired and awed me. The struggles he encountered, first while managing a foreign multinational, and then while starting and running his own companies in India, enlightened me; he always recounted the strifes with humor and met them with intelligence, determination and courage. I respectfully dedicate this book to my father, Dr C. Venkatesan (Papa), a fighter to the last.... the best of the Asian emperors.

Usha C. V. Haley
Chicago, May 1998

In addition to the above, I must thank my wife Siaw Peng for her understanding and tolerance for change, my children, Bryan, Melvyn and Stephanie for their high spirits in wanting to see one more book by their dad on the bookshelf. The last couple of months, with my new appointment at the Singapore Management University and this book project, my body and soul had been everywhere but with the family. Their support is most appreciated. Respectfully, I dedicate this book to a very special new Asian emperor, my father, Tan Thye Bee. Before he passed away, his deep involvement in the family business and the Chinese networks of South East Asia provided much insight to my understanding of the various issues discussed in the book.

Chin Tiong Tan
Singapore, May 1998

Part One

The Foundations of Understanding

Chapter One

An Introduction

'One generation passes away, and another generation comes; but the earth abides forever…. That which has been is what will be, that which is done is what will be done, and there is nothing new under the sun.'

Ecclesiastes

The above statement summarizes the history of the Overseas Chinese and the Chinese merchant classes. The Chinese merchant classes struggled against periodic campaigns of persecution in China to gain prosperity and their dreams of a good life for their families and children. The Overseas Chinese merchants struggled against periodic campaigns of persecution in their various new homelands to gain prosperity and their dreams of a good life for their families and children; and today, the Overseas Chinese struggle against periodic campaigns of persecution in many of their present homelands to gain their dreams of prosperity and a good life for their families and children. Though our book focuses on the corporate giants of the Overseas Chinese, we emphasize that the great majority of the Overseas Chinese who must face the travails of their people are not the super-rich Overseas Chinese of Asia, but those Overseas Chinese who are still struggling and basically, 'fighting the good fight'.

The Overseas Chinese, contrary to what the name would imply, do not form one people, but groups of diverse people. Like the mainland brethren they left behind, they differ by regional/cultural and linguistic groupings to a much greater degree than most US-born American citizens do, and almost as much physically as Americans do. Like the other great imperial populations of the latter twentieth century, Russia and the United States, the Chinese people, and particularly their overseas populations, have shown a great proficiency in creating and accumulating wealth when their governments permitted them to do so. This combination of courage, skills, and intelligence has created something which most of the Chinese emperors of the past passionately avoided, an overseas colonial empire. The colonial empire does not constitute the traditional political empire of old, but appears more akin to the economic empire which many accuse the United States of building. In some few instances such as Singapore and Taiwan (we will speak of Taiwan as an autonomous state although the mainland Chinese government considers it a province) the Overseas Chinese serve as this empire's political barons; but in every instance, they dominate as the commercial emperors of this New Asian Empire.

Westerners frequently view the Chinese people as one homogeneous population; and the Chinese as always having been under the sway of an all-powerful central imperial bureaucracy until the arrival of the Europeans. Neither of these two beliefs holds true. The Chinese people constitute a diverse population of different religions, different sub-cultures and different ethnic groups. Western China contains one of the earliest known, and best preserved burial sites of a Caucasian population anywhere in the world. The local population in the region continues to manifest some physical characteristics, for example, lighter, brown-colored hair and freckles, more frequently than the norm for other Asian populations.

Frequently, the Chinese Empire formed an empire in name only. Warlords from different areas would rise to challenge and sometimes to supplant the center. Invaders would breach Chinese defenses and create their own empires, introducing elements of their own cultures as they assimilated into the Chinese population. The center would collapse and China would break down into warring realms of various sizes and power; and frequently, the provinces would simply ignore the center's directives.

The merchant classes of the southern coastal regions would most frequently ignore the center's directives. These southern, coastal people dominated the various waves of Overseas Chinese who emigrated from China over the centuries. When the Chinese emperors periodically tried to block overseas commerce, contacts and emigration, the Southeastern Chinese provinces continued to press forward with their trading and emigration to wherever opportunities seemed to abound. In efforts to stop international trade and contacts, various Chinese emperors have embarked on the following prohibitive measures (this is a very short and incomplete list):

- In 1424, the Ming emperor, Hung-Hsi, banned foreign expeditions of any kind and scuttled an imperial fleet to emphasize his point.
- In 1661, the Manchu emperor, K'ang-hsi banned travel and evacuated coastal regions of China to about ten miles inland.
- In 1712, K'ang-hsi requested foreign governments to repatriate Chinese emigrants so that they could be executed.
- From 1717 until his death, K'ang-hsi tried once again and initiated a ban on travel. The emperor died in 1722, but his successors continued trying until 1727 when they lifted the ban after ten years of dismal failure.
- In 1959, Mao Tse-tung tried a new tack by calling on the Overseas Chinese to return home. Of the many millions of Overseas Chinese, Mao's ships picked up 100,000 seeking to come home.

In 1911, the Overseas Chinese communities finally responded in kind to the Manchu dynasty's many punitive campaigns and policies against them and their mainland brethren: they financed Sun Yat-sen's overthrow of the Manchus. The Overseas Chinese were, and remain, the epitome of capitalistic humanity.

The Overseas Chinese we have discussed and which form the focus of this book are these capitalist traders. Though people generally think of the Overseas Chinese as traders, other groups also make up the Overseas Chinese communities. Wang Gungwu (1991), in his book, *China and the Chinese Overseas*, discusses the four different patterns of Chinese migration. He identified the four patterns as:

- The trader pattern
- The coolie pattern
- The sojourner pattern, and
- The descent or re-migrant pattern

The trader pattern

The trader pattern represents those Chinese of commercial or professional classes who went overseas for reasons of business or employment. These people usually worked for their personal benefit or for domestic Chinese businessmen's benefits, usually, but not always, relatives of some sort. If their overseas efforts met with success, more relations and associates would follow and work to expand the businesses further.

The coolie pattern

The coolie pattern represents another group of Chinese who sought their fortune overseas. These individuals usually originated from the peasant classes, or were landless laborers, or the urban poor. They went overseas on labor contracts and many returned to China when their contracts came to an end. Many, however, stayed to build their fortunes, and their futures, in their new homes. This pattern has supplied the bulk of today's Overseas Chinese population.

The sojourner pattern

These members of the Overseas Chinese communities left China to act as representatives of the Chinese culture and way of life. They appeared during a period of time when Chinese governments were trying to re-exert their control over the increasingly wealthy Overseas Chinese communities. The sojourners perceived their duty as lobbying local governments for the rights to establish Chinese schools to educate the children of local Chinese in the Chinese language and in accordance with Chinese customs. They also sought to encourage local Overseas Chinese to remain faithful to their culture and country, and importantly, to their government.

The descent or re-migrant pattern

Growing numbers of Overseas Chinese do not speak the Chinese language, have never set foot in China, and have even emigrated from the countries in which their ancestors originally settled. These ethnic Chinese, socially and frequently even culturally, form members of their local national societies in every way imaginable.

Though we focus primarily on those Overseas Chinese who began to build their fortunes as merchants, the greatest number of today's Overseas Chinese commercial aristocracy in Southeast Asia descended from people who fit into the coolie and sojourner patterns. Regardless of which pattern the present-day Overseas Chinese businessmen and women descended from, they form supreme business practitioners, resourceful and daring, yet rarely so daring as to be foolhardy.

Who are the Overseas Chinese?

The bulk of Southeast Asians are, at least in part if not primarily, of Chinese origin (waves of Chinese emigration to the countries of Southeast Asia have occurred for literally thousands of years); yet, generally only those people migrating to Southeast Asia in the last one or two waves of migration are considered as Overseas Chinese. Most Southeast Asians considered Overseas Chinese arrived in their new homelands sometime in the latter years of the nineteenth century or in the twentieth century. Guangdong's and Fujian's coastal regions (to the immediate north and northeast of Hong Kong), as well as Hainan Island (between the Gulf of Tonkin and the South China Sea), dominated the last few waves of immigration. Figure 1.1 shows these coastal regions and the island. Eight primary groups of Chinese emigrated from these areas at this time (as enumerated by dialect and sub-dialect groupings) to the different countries of Southeast Asia.

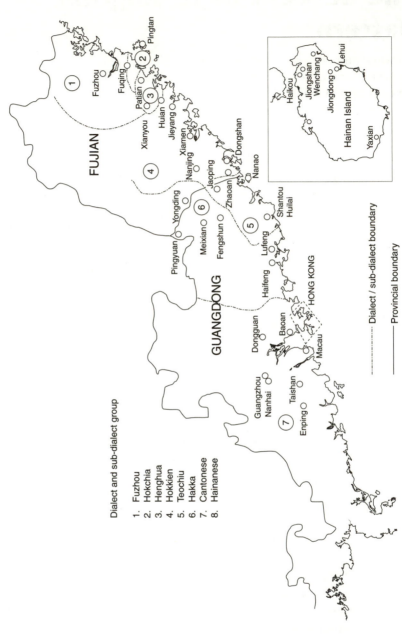

Figure 1.1 Primary homelands of today's Overseas Chinese. Adapted from East Asia Analytical Unit (1995)

Dialect and sub-dialect group

1. Fuzhou
2. Hokchia
3. Henghua
4. Hokkien
5. Teochiu
6. Hakka
7. Cantonese
8. Hainanese

------- Dialect / sub-dialect boundary

——— Provincial boundary

New Asian Emperors

They were the:

- Cantonese
- Fuzhou
- Hainanese
- Hakka
- Henghua
- Hokchia
- Hokkien
- Teochiu

When the different groups left China, they tended to settle among their own people in the different countries to which they went. Hence, one or two of the above-mentioned Chinese communities tend to dominate the Overseas Chinese populations of individual Southeast Asian countries. One or two of the linguistic groups may also dominate particular trades and professions. Table 1.1 presents the breakdown of the Overseas Chinese populations of the various Southeast Asian countries. For two countries, Cambodia and Myanmar, the figures form estimates. During the Pol Pot regime in Cambodia, the Chinese, primarily city dwellers, suffered especially badly and reliable figures for their population do not exist. Myanmar has never released reliable figures on their Overseas Chinese population.

As Table 1.1 shows, the Hokkien and Teochiu people tend to dominate in most Southeast Asian countries. Historical and geographical reasons contribute to this dominance. Throughout its history, China has alternated between outward-looking expansionist regimes and inward-looking isolationist regimes. The Hokkien and Teochiu homelands lacked good farmlands, and possessed relatively good ports on their coasts. Their physical distance from the different historical Chinese capitals also allowed them to escape the center's notice with the help of local authorities. Hence, under isolationist Chinese regimes that discouraged international trade and contacts, the Hokkien and Teochiu people could openly use their seafaring skills for domestic trade and fishing and had a substantial incentive to do so. Conversely, expansionist regimes that supported international trade also encouraged the Hokkien's and Teochiu's efforts to build trading relationships. Wealth would flow into these groups' homelands through their presence in Chinese trading circles. When circumstances changed again, and isolationists dominated policy, the Hokkien and Teochiu could not surrender the prosperity they had

Table 1.1 The Overseas Chinese in Southeast Asia

Country	Chinese as % of total pop.	Linguistic groups as a % of Chinese population					
		Hok	Can	Teo	Hak	Hai	Other
Brunei	16.0	+	+	0.0	+	0.0	0.0
Cambodia	2.0*	2.0	10.0	77.0	3.0	8.0	0.0
Indonesia	2.5	50.0	1.5	7.5	16.5	0.0	14.5
Laos	1.3	0.0	15.0	70.0	0.0	10.0	5.0
Malaysia	30.0	31.7	21.7	12.1	21.8	7.0	3.0
Myanmar	17.5*	30.0	20.0	0.0	0.0	0.0	50.0
Philippines	2.0	85.0	15.0	0.0	0.0	0.0	0.0
Singapore	77.6	40.0	18.0	23.0	9.0	7.0	3.0
Thailand	14.0	7.0	7.0	56.0	16.0	12.0	2.0
Vietnam	1.4	6.0	56.5	34.0	1.5	0.0	0.0
Taiwan	97.0	^					

Notes: Hok = Hokkien; Can = Cantonese; Teo = Teochiu; Hak = Hakka; Hai = Hainanese.

* These are very rough estimates.

+ While the Chinese population of Brunei is known, and it is known that it is dominated by the Hokkien, the precise breakdown is not known.

^ The Taiwanese population is predominantly Hokkien and the Taiwanese dialect is considered a variant of the Hokkien dialect. Though Taiwan is not a part of Southeast Asia, it is included due to its importance to the region through its cultural and economic ties.

gained through trade, and circumvented the central authorities whenever and however they could. With only subsistence farming possible, trade with other regions within China served essential needs for these groups. They used their domestic trade and shipping, and their contacts in local and central governments, to cover their activities and to maintain their international trading presence. The manner in which their international trading presence evolved had several important effects on the manner in which the Overseas Chinese have historically conducted their business.

In Table 1.1, the large 'Other' category for Myanmar arises because the largest group of ethnic Chinese in this country originates from traditional homelands spanning the common border of Myanmar and

Admiral Cheng Ho
Patron saint of Chinese trade and internationalism

The Ming emperor, Yung-lo (reign 1402–1424) constituted the last of the truly internationalist rulers among China's pre-communist rulers. The great admiral Cheng Ho served as the primary instrument of his international exploration and, to a limited extent, maritime imperialism. Cheng Ho was a eunuch of Mongolian ancestry and a Muslim who, during Yung-lo's reign, led six great voyages (he made a total of seven). The voyages averaged two years in length, and recorded visits to thirty countries, including visits to Hormuz at the entrance to the Red Sea, and to Jeddah, on the west coast of the Arabian Peninsula. Cheng Ho's voyages were not the sailing voyages of two or three lonely ships as were the European voyages of exploration; rather, they included major fleets with more than 20,000 men, upwards of sixty of the largest wooden capital ships ever made, with fleets of support vessels numbering more than 200 ships. During his trips, Cheng Ho established treaties with foreign powers such as Malacca (in present-day Malaysia), where he established a Chinese naval base, presented gifts to foreign rulers, and accepted tribute from them, collected many strange and exotic creatures for the Imperial menagerie, acquired new skills, and kept an eye out for new and potentially valuable trade goods and markets that Chinese merchants could profitably exploit. He also showed the military capability and skills of the Chinese navy by defeating and capturing or killing several rulers who challenged his fleet or refused to pay tribute to his Emperor – including the ruler of Ceylon, whom he deported to China after settling a pretender in his place; and the ruler of Sri Vijaya (in Sumatra), who was sent to China for execution (he was a Chinese pirate who had usurped the local throne). Cheng Ho's voyages ended upon the death of Yung-lo: during his short, year long reign, Yung-lo's son, Hung-hsi, made a clean sweep of various court factions and placed almost complete power firmly in the hands of the Confucian dominated bureaucracy. The bureaucracy ordered all imperial records of Cheng Ho's voyages to be destroyed.

Due to his accomplishments, Cheng Ho viewed his primary function as the development of trade and scholarship. Wherever you find large numbers of Overseas Chinese, you will find temples and/or statues dedicated to this patron saint of their enterprise and vision.

Table 1.2 The total and Chinese populations of Southeast Asia and Taiwan

	Total population[1]	Chinese population	% Chinese
Brunei	299,939	42,800	15.0
Cambodia	11,163,861	250,000[2]	2.0
Indonesia	209,774,138	5,244,353	2.5
Laos	5,116,959	66,520	1.3
Malaysia	20,491,303	6,147,391	30.0
Myanmar	46,821,943	8,193,840[2]	17.5
Philippines	76,103,564	1,522,071	2.0
Singapore	3,440,693	2,669,978	77.6
Thailand	59,450,818	8,323,115	14.0
Vietnam	75,123,880	1,051,734	1.4
Taiwan	21,699,776	21,048,783	97.0
Total	529,086,894	54,560,585	10.3

[1] Figures are compiled from the US Census Bureau, World Population Estimates and the East Asia Analytical Unit of the Australian Department of Foreign Affairs and Trade.
[2] These are very rough estimates.

China. The ethnic Chinese population in Myanmar's border with China has both historically lived in Myanmar and migrated across the poorly controlled border rathe than emigrating from the coastal regions of China.

Table 1.2 presents the total population of the countries under consideration, together with the total Chinese populations. The table clearly reveals the substantial populations of these countries. Indonesia alone forms the fourth most populous nation on earth. The proportion of the Overseas Chinese varies from nation to nation, but overall, remains relatively small at just over ten per cent. Though the Overseas Chinese form relatively small percentages of the local populations, they command their local economies.

Table 1.3 sketches the Overseas Chinese communities' economic influence in various Southeast Asian economies. As the table reveals, except in the Chinese-dominated countries, the economic participation of the Overseas Chinese in each country far outstrips their relative proportion of the population. Historically, several have recognized the Chinese merchant communities' energy and drive. One of Louis XV's ministers once complained that 'what France needs is a touch of the Chinese spirit' (Fernandez-Armesto, 1995, p. 296).

What is a network?

Most know that the Overseas Chinese operate in networks; but common perception erroneously assumes that these networks stem exclusively from clans or families. Trust constitutes the primary factor required for the formation of the networks, hence members of a

Table 1.3 Economic participation of the Overseas Chinese in Southeast Asian economies and Taiwan

Country	Chinese as % of population	% of market capital controlled by Chinese
Brunei	16.0	*
Cambodia	2.0[1]	70.0[2]
Indonesia	2.5	73.0
Laos	1.3	**
Malaysia	30.0	69.0
Myanmar	17.5[1]	**
Philippines	2.0	50–60.0
Singapore	77.6	81.0
Thailand	14.0	81.0
Vietnam	1.4	45.0[3]
Taiwan	97.0	95.0[4]

Notes: * In Brunei, Chinese often do not hold citizenship and businesses are held in partnerships with local citizens; ** Economies are just now moving out from under strict socialist systems; figures unavailable; [1] Very rough estimates; [2] Pre Pol Pot figure; [3] Estimate for Ho Chi Minh City only; [4] Per cent of economy controlled by ethnic Chinese, not market capitalization.
Source: Table compiled from *Far Eastern Economic Review*, February 26, 1998, and East Asia Analytical Unit estimates.

familial clan often form preferred members of networks. Three other traditional foundations for Overseas Chinese networks include the localities of origin, the dialects or sub-dialects spoken, and the traditional guilds (though one or a few locality based groups tend to dominate individual guilds). Increasingly, with the Overseas Chinese companies' growth, the Southeast Asian economies' enhanced complexity, the region's interconnectedness with other, global, economic regions, and more diverse and dispersed investments, simple trust is becoming the primary determinant of who is and is not a member of a network. Table 1.4 summarizes the different types and bases for the development of Overseas Chinese networks.

Ultimately, a 'Network' constitutes a tool. This tool builds trust, speeds decision making, facilitates high-quality decision making, builds customer satisfaction, and in the final analysis, generates competitive advantages for network members. These benefits accrue whether speaking of networks comprising separate and independent companies, or networks comprising executives within the same firms. Ram Charan (1991, p. 49) described networks in the following fashion:

> Networks are designed to empower managers to talk openly, candidly, and emotionally without fear, to enrich the quality of their decisions, to test each other's motives and build trust, and to encourage them to evaluate problems from the perspective of what is right for the customer and the company rather than from narrow functional or departmental interests.

He was referring to internal networks within firms; but, he could just as well have been referring to the external networks of the Overseas Chinese. The Overseas Chinese networks serve several functions. The networks consist of independent individuals of all kinds,

Table 1.4 Bases for Chinese networks

Network type	Basis for network
Clan grouping	By family surname
Locality grouping	By locality of origin in China
Dialect grouping	By dialect/sub-dialect spoken
Guild grouping	By craft practiced
Trust grouping	By prior experience/recommendation

businessmen and women from companies with and without any kind of ownership links, government bureaucrats, professionals and academics, private investors, and just friends.

On the surface, the Overseas Chinese form classic external networks. However, the networks also display an interconnectedness, derived from one of the four traditional bases for network formation listed in Table 1.4, which transform them into internal networks. An individual has a place within a clan, linguistic, locality or guild group, and also within the fifth, non-traditional trust group. Thus, the Overseas Chinese networks actually approximate external networks with some characteristics of internal networks.

Charan's categorizations of networks shed light on the Overseas Chinese networks. First, Charan stated that: 'Networks are designed to empower managers to talk openly, candidly, and emotionally without fear...' Family (clan), friendship (locality, linguistic or guild group) and trust form the building blocks of Overseas Chinese networks. Intense trust in the people with whom one deals enables one to communicate with them 'openly, candidly, and emotionally', without fear that what one tells them will be used to one's detriment or future embarrassment. Embarrassment forms an especial risk in Chinese societies that place great emphasis on 'face'. Thus, the networks constitute tools of empowerment for their members. The networks allow their members to discuss important pieces of information, and through this discussion, to generate the best possible decisions for the networks' managers and companies. As later chapters will elaborate, given Asia's business environments, informed decision-making forms a crucial benefit for members of the networks. In reality, strategic decisions sometimes go wrong, for both networks and non-network based institutions such as Western multinational corporations (MNCs). For example, Apple, at one time, dominated the personal computer industry, fought a valiant rearguard effort once IBM entered the business, but chose the wrong strategy and now has severe problems maintaining profitability. General Motors, still one of the world's greatest manufacturing concerns, is struggling to maintain market share. The Overseas Chinese firms have made similar strategic mistakes.

Second, Charan argued that with respect to their members, networks exist, 'to enrich the quality of their decisions'. This refers to the networks' abilities to transmit and to analyze information that considers the entire set of implications and meanings which accompany that information. Without the richness of openly available and/or acquirable information that managers can find in Western industrial democracies, information serves as a tremendous competitive advantage to companies operating in Asia. By depending upon, and expanding, abilities to acquire information through their networks, managers increase their chances of acquiring pieces of information that will resolve the business puzzles confronting them and give them tangible advantages against competitors.

Third, Charan stated that networks exist, 'to test each other's motives and build trust'. Both halves of this statement have crucial importance for the Overseas Chinese networks. For several reasons which we will consider later in the book when we discuss Chinese culture, members need to test trust in the networks. Importantly, trust does not constitute a transferable asset in the Chinese culture; consequently, Chinese business relationships often do not yield personal recommendations and endorsements. If one network member vouches for an outsider, then the network will give the outsider the benefit of the doubt, but only because the individual who gave the endorsement assumes responsibility for the outsider's trustworthiness. If the outsider fails the trust placed in him, he jeopardizes his honor as well as the honor and judgment of the individual who vouchsafed him. The endorsing member of the network will lose face and incur debt. Hence, networks' members test motives to build trust to where it can form the sole basis for substantial investment decisions.

Finally, Charan argued that for members, networks 'encourage them to evaluate problems from the perspective of what is right for the customer and the company rather than from narrow functional or departmental interests'. Though Overseas Chinese networks incorporate members who own or represent different, independent entities, this statement still has validity when one replaces the phrase, 'narrow functional or departmental interests', with 'narrow personal or company interests'. For an Overseas Chinese network to prosper and to continue, all its members participating in a particular business enterprise must benefit from that enterprise. Without that mutuality of benefit, essential mutuality of interest and trust cannot exist. The network will collapse in a frenzy composed of equal parts of vengeance for true and imagined deceits; and in networks' firms freezing into inaction due to inabilities to trust their information.

Mutualities of interest and trust increase when the networks consist of groups of people who, for the most part, have common experiences and world views, and who have worked successfully together, preferably over extended periods of time. Most networks' members also use mutuality of interest in another fashion. Mutuality of interest builds a focus for activities that eliminates the need to recheck constantly what other networks' members do in joint projects. This lax surveillance constitutes both a strength and a weakness. However trusted an individual, and consistent his past behaviors, potential gains or costs may tempt him to break with his network's partners or to break faith. Because of the high level of implicit trust in a network's members, the members can initially break faith without easy detection.

High costs can accrue to such breaches of faith especially if not detected quickly. An example of such lapses of faith came to light on June 25, 1997 when Thailand's new finance minister, Mr Thanong Bidaya, went to the Thai central bank with his top three aides and demanded to see its financial records. The collapse of the Thai Baht occurred seven days later on July 2, 1997 when the Thai government was forced to unpeg the Baht from the US dollar.

Prior to the crisis, the Thai finance ministry had guaranteed the Thai banks and financial institutions' financial creditworthiness. As some Thai institutions' creditworthiness became suspect due to increasingly high debt levels owed to foreign lenders, the finance ministry reiterated guarantees to calm local markets, foreign lenders and currency speculators. To ensure its ability to honor its guarantees, the finance ministry requested confirmation from the Thai Central Bank on the foreign currency reserves that the Bank held for the Thai government. The ministry, under Mr Thanong's predecessor, Mr Amnuay Viravan, could not get a response. Finally, Thailand's prime minister, Mr Chavalit Yongchaiyudh, lost patience and appointed Mr Thanong, president of the Thai Military Bank, as the new minister of finance. When he took office, Mr Thanong and his three top aides in the ministry immediately went to the currency office and personally inspected the Bank's books. What they found exceeded their worst nightmares. Reported reserves should have covered almost 60 days of Thai imports; in actuality, they could cover only two days' imports. The Central Bank's chief currency trader had tied up most of its currency reserves in forward contracts. Additionally, the Central Bank had already lent over US$8 billion to struggling Thai banks and finance companies. The largest Thai finance company, Finance One, was on the ropes and teetering badly even after having already received over US$1.4 billion in government loans. With no more funds to lend, the finance ministry informed Finance One and selected news media that no more funds were forthcoming. The same message went out to fifteen other troubled financial institutions. The Central Bank's officers had not reported the true state of affairs six months earlier to the government and public because the officers would have lost face. When the ministry's call for confirmation of foreign currency holdings arrived, the Central Bank's officers could not bear to lose face by admitting their losses, and simply refused to respond. When the new finance minister came and inspected the books personally, the game was up. He transmitted his findings to the government. The revelations shattered the Thai people's as well as local and foreign investors' confidence, led to the Thai economy's and financial markets' collapse, and eventually to the East Asian currency and financial crisis.

While Charan adequately presented the network organization's benefits, important flaws exist in his thesis. Charan stated (p. 52), 'Companies don't build networks so that managers will "like" or behave like "family".' In truth, companies don't build networks at all, people do. Companies can build teams, and teams can prove enormously effective management tools, but teams are not networks. Companies can also create environments to formally recognize networks and to encourage them to flourish, and by so doing, use networks to help accomplish the companies' goals and objectives.

In actuality, networks have always existed within companies, whether in Asia, Africa, Europe, or the Americas. The networks have historically been informal networks of individual executives and blue-collar employees (usually composed exclusively of one or the other type of employee). These networks generally consisted of friends and associates within the companies and most frequently formed informal communications networks that more than rivaled the companies' own formal communications networks in efficiency and influence. As the networks formed informal and unrecognized organizations, companies rarely used them deliberately in their plans. In fact, if the companies adopted policies that network members perceived as seriously detrimental to the interests of one, a few, or all the networks' members, the networks would frequently move to frustrate the senior management's plans and goals. The key elements in these networks' development, however, involved a perceived mutuality of interest, trust, and, if not friendship, some reciprocal respect. Companies cannot build networks because they cannot mandate the creation of trust, friendship or respect. As noted earlier, companies may build teams, and within teams, networks may arise. However, teams cease to exist once companies decide to use team members for other projects and reassign them. Networks appear much more permanent – they continue after projects end. Networks also serve their own purposes when team members are formally working together, and beyond.

This discussion of the Overseas Chinese networks emphasizing personal trust and the facilitation of transactions between limited numbers of favored individuals and companies may seem to approximate the Godfather trilogy of movies. However, the Overseas Chinese networks are not criminal organizations, just organizations of people who historically could rely on no one but themselves, or on no organizations or institutions but their own.

In our earlier historical discussion of the various Chinese governments' isolationist tendencies, we indicated that the networks maintained China's international trade presence; and, the networks, through their contacts, knowledge and information, frustrated the central governments' attempts to cut China off from the world entirely. The networks played similar roles in the communist era. In a different way, although the present Chinese government has a definitely internationalist orientation, the networks are playing similar roles today.

Next, we will discuss the role of the Overseas Chinese in Southeast Asia and the world economy. In Chapter Three, we will compare the two pre-eminent Oriental Asian cultures of China and Japan to understand better the Chinese business culture's origin and to see why the networks, which thwarted the central Chinese authorities' wishes, never arose to challenge seriously Japanese central authorities.

The role of the Overseas Chinese in Southeast Asia

As we noted above, the Overseas Chinese play a substantial economic role in Southeast Asia. This role goes significantly beyond the

Networks in history:
a partial list of networks which have influenced business over
time

The Overseas Chinese networks that form the subject of this book, have received much media attention and have influenced greatly Southeast and East Asia's economic and business development. Yet, they form one of myriad networks. Networks have existed throughout history. We present here some past- and present-day networks.

- *The Overseas Indian networks*: The Overseas Indian networks form a growing force in Southeast Asia and elsewhere. They show many of the same managerial traits as the Overseas Chinese with a slightly greater tendency to depend on family members and friends as the source of their network partners. Indian networks also tend to have less diversified investments than the Overseas Chinese.
- *The Hispanic grupos*: The Hispanic *grupos* serve as competent and fierce competitors. They develop through family and friendship ties. The *grupo* usually centers around a major enterprise. Growth appears diversified, but usually follows some form of backward or forward expansion up or down value chains. Once the *grupo* builds two or more companies of substantial size, the companies may spin off. The famous Monterrey Group of companies in Mexico represents just such a pattern among its component *grupos*.
- *The old school tie*: Though possibly losing influence, old school tie networks have played a tremendous role in the United Kingdom's and United States' economic and business development. Most premier university programs in the two countries offered, and still do, more than just a good education. The universities offer ways to meet and to build bonds of friendship and trust with other members of society with the education, training and mutuality of interests to advance the nations' economies without seriously endangering the social status quo. As educational levels within the countries improve and become more generally available to the masses, and as the two countries continue to push globalization, the old school tie networks have not only proven their effectiveness, but have

weakened their influence within their home countries.

■ *Japanese inter- and intra-firm networks*: Most Western businesspeople have heard of the inter-firm Japanese networks, the *keiretsu*. These organizations have proven ferocious competitors in the international arena. Despite present difficulties in the Japanese economy, the best of the non-traditional *keiretsus*, formed around companies such as Sony, Toyota and Honda, continue with strategies to maintain their competitive positions regardless of governmental actions. Many may not know that many of the major Japanese companies also promote the creation of class-based (class-based refers to the graduation year in which the executive was hired) networks within their managerial groups. The companies promote the creation of these networks by not promoting individuals in the early years of their careers, but by promoting entire classes at once. Thus, with the promotion of any one individual depending on the success of all, the individuals have incentives to work together.

■ *The criminal networks*: Criminal networks exist in all societies and countries. They have irretrievably negative effects and represent a substantial tax on legitimate businesses.

■ *Secret societies*: Secret societies, influential throughout the history of the Overseas Chinese, also constitute networks and exist in all societies and nations. The Masonic Order and Opus Dei form two particularly influential secret societies in Western countries.

■ *The Islamic clans*: Western concepts of nationhood did not exist in the early Islamic period. The early Arabian empires centered in Damascus, and later in Baghdad and Cordoba, drew on personal loyalties by networks of individuals and clans owed to increasingly fewer and more influential Islamic clans and individuals until finally reaching the central focus of the royal family and the Caliph.

■ *The feudal system*: The feudal system of Europe formed one of the most successful network systems of all time. It maintained and enhanced European civilization through difficult periods with substantial degrees of uncertainty and danger, and significant chances that European society, as a whole, would collapse entirely.

numbers in Table 1.3. The Overseas Chinese serve as facilitators for much of the flow of trade and investment in Southeast Asia. Through their traditionally high savings rates and financial institutions, the Overseas Chinese contribute the capital that funds investment and growth; through their distribution channels and retail institutions, they provide the goods that satisfy the needs and wants of local populations; through their philanthropy and social organizations they manufacture the very limited safety nets that the poor in Southeast Asia have; and through the philosophical, social and cultural organizations, transmitted for centuries through migrants from China, they have helped to render cohesion and social structures for the people of Southeast Asia to withstand successfully the onslaught of colonial cultures and to maintain their cultural identities. We will now proceed to consider the aforementioned issues in greater detail.

The Overseas Chinese maintain among the highest savings rates in the world. Because of their history, the Overseas Chinese believe in two basic strategies. First, they keep significantly larger proportions of their capital in liquid form than most would consider desirable in the West. Second, they have historically believed in spreading their investments widely, making sure that the loss of single investments will not severely damage their financial positions. Their high savings rates generally ensure that their well-managed financial institutions can withstand even the worst economic periods. Today, substantial concerns exist about the severe weakness of Asian financial institutions from Japan to Indonesia. Yet, despite the problems besetting the region, banks from Taiwan, Hong Kong and Singapore have maintained their economic strength and seem poised to survive and to prosper through the present economic crisis. Even with the Singaporean market's small size and the upstart Peregrine Fund's collapse (the Fund grew spectacularly by backing investments that traditional institutions declined), traditional financial and banking institutions have remained strong.

Though not consistently throughout the region, the Overseas Chinese prefer to maintain control over the distribution of their goods. Perhaps this practice originates through their historical role in the trade and distribution of goods; however, regardless of the reason, most goods sold in Southeast Asia pass through the hands of Overseas Chinese intermediaries at some time between manufacturers and end users. Hence, due to the lack of market data in the region, the Overseas Chinese merchants of the region define, to a great extent, the perceived needs and wants of the region's markets.

Philanthropy forms one of the basic tenets of Confucianism. Successful people have duties to provide charitable contributions of goods, services and cash. Throughout Southeast Asian countries, one encounters hospitals funded primarily through Chinese social organizations' contributions, free and subsidized food and medications distributed by Chinese merchants and associations during periods of severe economic dislocation (as happened in Indonesia during the difficulties of 1997 and 1998), and various other kinds of charitable activities. In the 1950s, Chinese societies all over Asia contributed to the founding of a Chinese university – Nanyang University in Singapore. Especial efforts exist to relieve the suffering of the elderly, for whom the Chinese have a deep respect.

As we noted previously, many waves of Chinese immigrants entered Southeast Asia over the centuries. Myriad other influences have also merged together to form local Southeast Asian cultures. If one considers the situation found in Malaysia, the truth of Southeast Asia becomes evident. The Overseas Chinese make up a substantial minority population of about 30 percent of the population. The government and the majority of the citizens consider Malaysia an Islamic country, yet the government permits their Chinese population to send their children to Chinese schools (though it does so under increasingly more stringent limitations). Side by side with Islamic mosques, one finds Chinese and Hindu temples, and Malay, Chinese and Indian (another substantial minority) social organizations inextricably intertwined in providing services to the Malaysian populace. The Chinese philosophical, social and cultural organizations did not solely provide the cohesion and social structures that enabled the Southeast Asian people to withstand colonial onslaughts and to maintain their cultural identities; yet, they exercised at least as much influence as any other Asian culture and institution in doing so.

The role of the Overseas Chinese worldwide

The Overseas Chinese play a large and ever-widening role in the international arena. Among the brands of Overseas Chinese companies, one finds such names as Acer Computers, the largest presence in the computer industry of any company headquartered outside of the United States or Japan; Creative Technology, which holds the dominant market-share position in the computer sound card industry with its Sound Blaster brand; Asia Brewery and Asia Pacific Breweries (brewer of Tiger Beer), both of which are locked in an increasingly fierce contest for dominance of the Southeast Asian market with San Miguel (not an Overseas Chinese company); Tiger Medical, makers of Tiger Balm; several banking concerns, such as United Overseas Bank, Overseas Chinese Banking Corporation, Hong Leong Bank and Dao Heng Bank; hotel and resort properties, such as Shang-ri-La Hotels; industrial concerns such as Formosa Plastics; and even some Chinese companies engaged in overseas trading, the business which created the wealth of the great Overseas Chinese companies, such as Kuok Brothers, which at one time controlled 10 percent of the world's sugar trade.

The Overseas Chinese role in international trade, however, goes beyond the companies that they personally control. The Overseas Chinese form a tremendous conduit between Western companies and the liberalizing, formerly communist countries of Asia. Through their contacts within the governments of these countries, and their networks within those countries, they frequently facilitate investments that could languish due to a clash of cultures and lack of knowledge. An example of such an occurrence happened when Daimler-Benz asked the government of Singapore to intercede on its behalf with the government of Vietnam. Daimler-Benz was stuck with a significant sunk cost in an investment in Vietnam that had stalled for an extended period of time. The Singaporean government, due to its Singapore, Inc. self-image as middleman to the world (as described in Haley, Low and Toh, 1996), actually constitutes one of the great Overseas Chinese enterprises. Soon after that request, Singapore's senior minister, Mr Lee Kwan Yew, visited Vietnam and got the investment back on track for Daimler-Benz.

Figure 1.2   Howqua – The Great Official

Wu Ping-Chien (The Great Official) – ideal of the Chinese merchant class

Wu Ping-Chien, better known as Howqua, Chinese for the Great Official, was probably the richest man in the world during a time of true financial giants. He prospered during a period of time when the Astors and Rothschilds dominated and Jim Bowie was the largest single private landholder in the known world. During the first half of the nineteenth century, Howqua controlled the greatest part of all the world's trade with China. As China would not permit the importation of any bulk items from other countries, the traders came to Howqua with silver and gold. Howqua had a reputation for scrupulous honesty and tremendous generosity. When American traders with whom he had conducted business in the past offered him promissory notes, he tore them up and reminded them that he knew them as honest men. When prices for goods that he was purchasing rose after the signing of the contracts, he paid the new, higher prices. He fought valiantly and, in the end, futilely, to stop the British from smuggling opium into China. He paid a substantial portion of the reparations which China was forced to pay after the opium wars out of his own pocket after already having paid for the improvement of Chinese fortifications before the war. He paid for a thousand and one public benefits and infrastructural improvements in Canton, his home province, and through all this, he suffered the persecution and ridicule of the Chinese bureaucracy's Confucian mandarins. The mandarins falsely charged his son with opium smuggling and gave Ping-Chien the nickname, Howqua, or Great Official. The title served as a prestigious honorific for a bureaucrat, but only as mockery for Ping-Chien, a member of the merchant class, the lowest of Chinese social classes. Ultimately, of all the Great Officials of China in the last century, history remembers only Howqua, the greatest of the Chinese merchants. His portraits hang in many places, including the East India Hall of Fame in Salem Massachusetts, where one may see the accompanying portrait.

Following chapters

In our succeeding chapters, we present a short discussion of Confucianism, its centrality to Chinese culture and life, and its impact on traditional Chinese business philosophy and practice. We then discuss how the history of the Overseas Chinese has combined with Confucianism and their environments to mold the people one meets and does business with today. In the process, we describe the present strategic decision-making environment in Asia, and its evolution. Next, we describe the decision-making of the Overseas Chinese. Though many say the Overseas Chinese do no strategic planning, we will explain the basic concepts and philosophy which underlie their decision-making, and demonstrate its similarity to well accepted Western conceptualizations of strategic planning. We conclude by discussing the implications of the Overseas Chinese model of planning for their strategic partners and competitors. In doing so, we present the views on strategic planning and decision-making held by some of the most influential and private of the New Asian Emperors together with those of leading members of the next generation.

Chapter Two

Confucianism +:

the philosophical and cultural roots of the Overseas Chinese

'No one likes Confucius before they come to power. Once they do, they begin to see his good side.'

Kong Fanyin (a present-day descendent of Confucius)

Introduction

In the above statement, Kong Fanyin spoke one of the great truisms of Asian political and business life. Confucius opposed rebellion against a legitimate prince under any circumstance. The second great sage of Confucianism, Mencius, introduced the idea that a prince can behave in so improper a manner as to justify the masses' overthrowing their rightful prince. In either case, both great sages preferred compromise and conciliation to confrontation just as the New Asian Emperors often do.

A decade ago, very few studies existed of non-Japanese Asian business groups; these studies catered to small groups of scholars actively studying Asian business practices without gaining much attention from the business community at large. However, in the last few years, a number of studies have appeared that trace these Asian business groups' growing influence and development (e.g. Hamilton, 1996; Khanna and Palepu, 1997; Redding, 1995, 1996; Shigematsu, 1994). Many of these studies have questioned the simplistic descriptions of Asian and Overseas Asian business firms that accompanied Asia's early economic development. Some recent scholars have claimed that many earlier studies err by emphasizing Confucianism; these scholars have stated that more modern and specifically economic philosophical systems of behavior have replaced the old, traditional systems (Hamilton, 1996). But on inspecting their claims and explanations, the errors in these scholars' arguments become apparent. In this chapter we will discuss Confucian, Buddhist and Taoist economic and behavioral principles to gain a greater understanding of their implications for business practices in the region. In later chapters, we will elaborate on the Overseas Chinese companies' present-day practices and demonstrate the traditional philosophies' influence on them.

A relatively unsuccessful itinerant teacher and government bureaucrat named K'ung Fu-tzu (later latinized to Confucius) had a cosmic effect on Chinese societal and cultural development. His dramatically profound influence, and that of his greatest adherent, Mang-tsze K'o (later latinized to Mencius and sometimes referred to as the Second Sage), on China and the Chinese culture, though dimly recognized and often misunderstood by non-Chinese, is apparent to the New Asian Emperors. Indeed, Robert Kuok, Malaysia's great Overseas Chinese tycoon, in a 1985 speech to the World Management Congress said, 'As children, we learned about moral values – mainly Confucian.'

Confucius, and especially his successor, Mencius, waged a philosophical war for the heart and soul of China's spiritual development. Their victory created a humanistic philosophy and outlook on life that believed in hard work; conservative adherence to traditional values; the dominance of society over individual and family over society; and a society in which there is a place for everyone, and everyone has his or her place and role to play in society. Though the West knows little of Mencius, who lived some 100 years after Confucius, they know much more of Confucius through Mencius' interpretations of his writings than through anything that Confucius communicated directly. One can attribute the development of Confucianism to Mencius' championing of the inherent goodness of man, something that Confucius neglected to address.

As the '+' in this chapter's title indicates, besides Confucianism, Buddhism and Taoism represent two other strong influences on Chinese culture and society. These three streams of thought fused together to form the Chinese view of man's place in society and influenced the Chinese character's and personality's development. The four men at the center of these enormously influential philosophies, the Buddha, Confucius, Mencius, and Lao Tzu were not messengers from heaven or prophets; they were philosophers who felt they had discovered important perspectives on living good lives. Confucius and Lao Tzu probably formed contemporaries in ancient China; Mencius lived in China about a hundred years later; and the historians have documented well the Buddha's life in India in the fifth and fourth centuries, BC. Though Westerners often think otherwise, and Taoism and Buddhism have evolved into religions, none of the four saw themselves as founders of religions but only as teachers of a philosophy of life, something which Confucius, Mencius and Lao Tzu referred to sparsely as 'The Way'. The four recognized the importance of the 'heavens' in life, but never defined the heavens; they merely accepted the heavens that their societies had defined.

The Overseas Chinese have cast off many of the elements within the streams of thought that historically limited Chinese economic development (Redding, 1993); however, the basic economic and behavioral tenets that flowed from these philosophies influence their business practices today. First, though they have circumscribed these philosophies' limiting influences, their perceptions of the ideals in human behavior, and frequently their interpretations of other persons' behaviors, remain rooted in their philosophical traditions. Second, the development of the Overseas Chinese has resulted from the creative tensions and conflicts between the influence of these philosophical schools on Chinese culture, life and governance on one side – and human nature and their lives' practical necessities and experiences on the other. However, these philosophies fail to incorporate human nature's economic aspects into their tenets of behavior, presenting us with several paradoxes, and with some of the greatest differences between Western and Chinese societies.

Confucianism offers a prescription for the proper behaviors of men, and especially for members of the gentlemanly classes, in their interactions with society, their peers, and their princes. The philosophy places its entire emphasis on human behaviors and man's place in society. (Through the balance of our examples and text on Confucianism, we use male pronouns. Confucian philosophy is inherently sexist, and focused almost exclusively on the father as the central figure. This male-dominated perspective on life viewed females as subordinate to males, and continues to do so today.) Within

Confucius' writings, some passages address natural or godly phenomena and human nature; however, he does not place them at the center of his philosophical deliberations. The central role in Confucian philosophy goes to human social interactions. This characteristic Confucian approach appears in Book 5, Chapter 12 of *The Analects*:

> Tzu-kung said, Our Master's views concerning culture and the outward insignia of goodness, we are permitted to hear; but about Man's nature and the ways of Heaven he will not tell us anything at all.

Buddhism and Taoism both emphasize the oneness of nature and mankind's position within that oneness; yet they also fail to incorporate the practical, economic aspects of human nature in their prescriptions for behaviors considered desirable within that oneness. Buddhism emphasizes creating an ideal of human nature – a goal which people can achieve through learning and acts of will. Taoism focuses on the paradoxical duality of all nature, and gaining an understanding of nature through knowledge of that duality and its implications.

Confucianism, Buddhism and Taoism refuse to pander to mankind's inherent greed, desires for independence, success, and recognition, and preferences for reacting directly to external stimuli. The philosophies acknowledge the basic, economically practical aspects of human nature, view them as undesirable, and attempt to do away with them. Conversely, philosophers with analogous influences on Western culture, thought and behavior, from ancient Greece and the Age of Reason, recognize and incorporate human nature's underlying, economically practical aspects into their basic tenets of desirable behavior rather than reject it. The Western philosophers seek to exploit the directional thrust of human nature's practical, economic aspects and to focus it towards socially desirable goals such as wealth creation for society as a whole, reduction of human suffering through charitable contributions and utilization of personal wealth for societal good.

Significant differences exist between the Confucian, Buddhist and Taoist approaches to mankind's economic nature. Though traditionally rejecting the more economically practical aspects of human nature, the philosophies have incorporated unique reactions to them. For example, Buddhism rejects acquisition entirely when prescribing the ideal in human behavior. Taoism, though not rejecting acquisition outright, through its perspective of nature's paradoxical duality, argues that wealthy men should not acquire more, but should want less. Individuals wanting less will always have sufficient means to obtain what little they want and maintain a surplus; hence such individuals will always have more wealth than the individuals wanting more, acquiring more, and never seeming to have enough to obtain everything they want. The Overseas Chinese have altered this important perspective to their own use and benefit: they generally live frugal lives relative to their incomes and have high savings rates. For example, in 1996, New Asian Emperor, Li Kai Shang, with estimated assets of US$8 billion, was finally persuaded by his son Victor to change his 20-year-old Mercedes for a Nissan President. Li also owns a 19-year-old Rolls-Royce for driving his guests through town. In public he wears a Citizen wristwatch that cost him US$50.

China's most influential philosophers' classic works form a surprisingly small body. *The Analects* of Confucius constitutes an extremely short masterpiece, readable in a few hours. Lao Tzu presented his philosophies in two books, the *Tao Ching* and the *Te Ching*, now united into the *Tao Te Ching*, or the *Book of Tao*, containing a series of very short chapters, some of them only three or four lines long. Although also of limited quantity, more exists of Mencius' writings than of either of his predecessors. Confucius' and Mencius' philosophies are presented, much as Plato's was, as conversations between the master and his students or between contemporaries, or simply as their statements.

Few scholars today seriously doubt the basic intent of Confucius' writings. Yet, serious schisms in interpretation occurred in the past, the most serious during Mencius' time. The schisms focused upon the effects that basic beliefs on men's natures would have on the interpretation of Confucian thought. Mencius championed the basic underlying goodness of mankind. He argued that, left to their own devices and inherent natures, men would develop as good beings, and that Confucian thought and philosophy should be interpreted from this perspective. He believed that evil men had their inherently good natures corrupted by their environments. His two great contemporaries both held views which outraged Mencius' high moral perspective; if their philosophies had gained the upper hand, the interpretation of Confucianism, and especially of Neo-Confucianism which later took hold, would have differed profoundly from today. Confucius himself only addressed the how of things – the practical side of men's behaviors and interactions with society. Confucius rarely addressed anything as nebulous and irrelevant as men's underlying natures.

Yang Chu formed the first of Mencius' great contemporaries, and the one whose philosophies he most despised. Yang Chu, a Confucian, pressed the argument of extreme egoism. He argued that men had primary moral duties to survive as long and as comfortably as possible. He did not include a concept of charity or self-sacrifice in his philosophy. Extreme and incorrect interpretations of some chapters in Lao Tzu's work the *Tao Te Ching*, often quite obscure, may have influenced him. For example, Chapter 5, book 1, of Lao Tzu's *Tao Te Ching* reads:

> Heaven and earth are ruthless, and treat the myriad creatures as straw dogs*; the sage is ruthless, and treats the people as straw dogs. Is not the space between heaven and earth like a bellows?
>> It is empty without being exhausted:
>> The more it works the more comes out.
>> Much speech leads inevitably to silence.
>> Better to hold fast to the void.

If one take's heaven's behavior as the ideal, then one should behave in a ruthless fashion, without showing charity. One should also never contribute all to society, either through self-sacrifice or through performances for the public good. Hence, Yang Chu's conclusion that self-sacrifice brings destruction, charity brings abuse, and the best goals involve clinging to the voids that surround individuals, surviving as long and as best as possible and exploiting every situation for personal gain. Yang Chu's philosophy seems remarkably similar to the Michael Douglas character's philosophy in the movie, *Wall Street*, where in a speech he proclaimed: 'Greed is Good!'

Yang Chu's philosophy had little influence on Mencius' Confucian economic philosophy. However, immense similarities exist between the economic philosophy of Confucius and Mencius and that of socialism. Thus, for Asia's communist countries, unlike for the Soviet

---

* Straw dogs were temple offerings. Prior to the offering they were treated with great deference; afterwards they were trampled into the ground.

Union, socialism did not constitute the short-term grafting of a foreign ideology onto society. To a great extent, socialism re-established traditional economic philosophies that dominated the region, except during the short hiatus of Dr Sun Yat Sen's Chinese Republic. Often the communist system just used new names for old concepts. Hence, the assumption that Asian communist governments and parties will suffer the same, almost overnight, collapse that they suffered in the Soviet Union and Eastern Europe appears mistaken.

Mo Tzu, a charismatic philosopher and leader, formed the second of Mencius' great antagonists; his movement collapsed soon after his death. Mo Tzu led a universal love movement, surprisingly similar to the one experienced in the West in the 1960s. He argued that man's greatest duty involved living life to promote the free exchange of love between humans, and treating all countries as one's own. Mo Tzu, like the universal love advocates of the 1960s, advocated extreme pacifism. Mencius scorned Mo Tzu's philosophy: he felt that universal love removed families from the center of men's lives, and would require that men not love and honor their own fathers above all other people.

Confucius never lived to see his great influence, but Mencius did. Mencius vanquished his philosophical opponents and observed his philosophy of Confucian humanism and human nature's essential goodness triumph. Though Mencius enjoyed limited success in his political career, he could collect sufficient wealth by serving his Chinese princes to retire to a life surrounded by students and to prepare his great works for publication. Confucius, on the other hand, died as he had lived, an itinerant teacher, philosopher and government bureaucrat. His students worshipped him, other thinkers and educated people respected and esteemed him; but the Chinese princes of his day failed to champion him.

The Buddha – prince among saints – saint among princes

The Buddha was born around 566 BC into a princely Hindu family which ruled from its capital city, Kapilavastu; he died around 483 BC. His true name was Siddhartha. He enjoyed a traditional upbringing and the first 29 years of his life appear

---

entirely unremarkable. When he was 29, however, he abandoned his home and family, including his wife and new-born son, and embarked upon a life as a wandering ascetic. For several years, he tried many of the traditional activities undertaken by Indian ascetics including various penances, programs of austerity and self-denial, and came away disappointed and unenlightened. With this initial failure, he turned to meditation. His still famous seven-week period of meditation under the Bo tree had better results. He came away enlightened and with his philosophy firmly developed. He concluded that all unhappiness and suffering were rooted in desires, which were in turn rooted in ignorance; the true path to *Nirvana*, or salvation, lay in mastering and conquering desires. He taught that as one progressed through rebirths, the soul's success in reaching *Nirvana* came through practicing the Noble Eightfold Path which comprised: Right Aspirations, Right Conduct, Right Effort, Right Livelihood, Right Meditation, Right Mindfulness, Right Speech, and Right Views. Once he established his philosophy and teachings, he reverted to an itinerant ascetic; however, now, he preached his philosophy, and the people who listened to his teachings called him the Buddha, or the Enlightened One. From the time of his enlightenment to his death, the Buddha traversed northern India, spreading his message, and founding orders of monks and nuns. His new orders originated as mendicants, but over time formed monasteries, formalized the Buddha's teachings and philosophy, and founded the first great centers of learning in India to promulgate the Buddha's philosophy to the public. Rather than the founder of a new religion, the Buddha viewed himself as a Hindu reformer. He championed many revolutionary reforms including creating orders of nuns, and rejecting the caste system, which had become increasingly rigid and oppressive with the Brahmin castes' domination of traditional Hinduism. The Mauryan emperor, Ashoka, became one of the new philosophy's greatest converts: he sent out its early missionaries to spread Buddhism into China and Southeast Asia thereby ensuring its survival, success and influence.

Confucianism's influence on Overseas Chinese trade and economics

Confucianism's most apparent influence on Chinese economic culture deals with perceptions of the merchant classes and profit motives: Confucianism frowned on both. The Confucian philosophers viewed the mobile, merchant classes with suspicion and considered them the lowest class of humanity. The philosophers, conversely, exalted peasants, who were tied to the land. The Chinese peasantry, though immobile, did not approximate Russian serfs or Spanish peons; their attachment to the land arose because their income originated from their work on the soil. This inability to transfer livelihoods meant that the government could locate peasants to tax them, to draft them into work projects, and to use them to fill the army's ranks. The peasants' livelihoods depended on their staying in known locations; and on the government's abilities to provide the peasants with safe, stable environments at those specific locations. As the government's bureaucracy and army provided these safe, stable environments – and the peasants' taxes supported the bureaucracy and army – Confucian philosophers viewed the peasants and the government as having mutual interests. In short, the government could easily control the peasants because they lacked mobility and needed the government's services.

The Confucian perspective on society also contributed to their philosophers' perceptions on the peasants' inherent controllability. The philosophers envisioned appropriate places and roles for everyone in society, and they saw these roles as good for individuals and society. Mencius taught this philosophy in the following way as the basis for good rule (p. 62, *Lau*, 1995):

> There are affairs of great men, and there are affairs of small men. Moreover, it is necessary for each man to use the products of all the hundred crafts. If everyone must make anything he uses, the Empire will be led along the path of constant toil. Hence it is said, 'There are those who use their minds and there are those who use their muscles'. The former rule; the latter are ruled. Those who rule are supported by those who are ruled.

The above idea that rulers must control small men runs throughout Confucian philosophy. This emphasis on control of the lesser by the greater introduces acceptance of authoritarianism into the Chinese mindset that Western managers or political figures rarely find among their subordinates. However, today, many Overseas Chinese companies that retain Confucian practices are encountering problems recruiting professional managers. Few bright young managers want to work for companies that will never give them roles in formulating corporate strategies because of their age. In many Overseas Chinese firms, respect for authority and age too often also rules out any criticism of the boss. However, importantly, Confucian superiors, or great men, had to use their authority for the benefit of small men, and to do so with as little force as possible; the Confucians perceived small men, or those of subordinate classes, as incapable of governing their own actions. (The passage below uses the term 'gentleman'. The Confucian gentlemen served as courtier in the courts of the rulers, and as advisors and educators of the royal young. Bloodlines or force did not restrict membership; rather, membership depended upon individuals' levels of educational attainment, their training in the social graces, and in the rituals and behaviors necessary for life at court.) Mencius expressed this aspect of rule in the following manner (p. 60, *Lau*, 1995):

> Only a gentleman can have a constant heart in spite of a lack of a constant means of support. The people, on the other hand, will not have constant hearts if they are without constant means. Lacking constant hearts they will go astray and fall into excesses, stopping at nothing. To punish them after they have fallen foul of the law is to set a trap for the people. How can a benevolent man in authority allow himself to set a trap for the people?

This statement explains the Confucian perspective on the relationships between individuals in authority and subordinates; as well as the Confucian economic perspective that we will now discuss.

The Confucians frowned upon merchants and discriminated against them for exactly the opposite reasons that they exalted peasants. Merchants enjoyed mobility that contributed to their livelihoods. By locating and transporting goods across locations, merchants earned their profits. However, this mobility meant that the government could not depend on the merchants. For example, merchants could avoid military service by moving their goods and families to other locations.

Merchants could also avoid taxes by hiding earnings in neighboring territories. The merchants did not need the government's safe and stable environment for their livelihoods; if the environment became too dangerous, merchants could move their livelihoods. In other words, the government could not control the merchants as completely as they did the peasants. The Confucian mandarins' perceptions of peasants and merchants resembled communists' perceptions of workers and capitalists: they exalted and controlled the former, they demonized and persecuted the latter.

Confucianism also viewed the profit motive as corrupt. For example, Confucius said (Book 4, No. 16, p. 24, Waley, 1996), 'A gentleman takes as much trouble to discover what is right as lesser men take to discover what will pay.' In his introduction to Waley's translation, Robert Wilkinson gave another, more damning interpretation of this passage and other related ones, 'The lack of moral principle manifests itself in various forms of egotism but principally as greed: while the gentleman does what is right, the small, or lesser man only considers what is profitable.' This theme runs consistently throughout Confucianism.

Latter day neo-Confucian mandarins during the Ming and Manchu dynasties may have also viewed the merchant classes as potential threats to their power. Mencius' statement quoted above damned the merchants from two different perspectives. First, the government could not depend on independent merchants to 'support those who rule'. Second, merchants primarily used their mind, not their muscles; as the merchants could also provide small men with the goods necessary to pacify them, one could argue that the merchants should rule, not the mandarins and their princes.

Mencius indirectly acknowledged the merchants' importance as those who arranged for the exchanges necessary for 'one man to use the products of all the hundred crafts'. The merchants also often had financial strength. Thus they would have represented a substantial, legitimate threat to the mandarins.

Confucianism emphasized the ability to control as it rejected loyalty to the government for patriotic reasons; it opposed the strong patriotism that has caused such tremendous pain and suffering in more modern times. To Confucius and his followers, families rather than states provided the basis for society: the duty owed by sons to their fathers assumed primary importance; for gentlemen, the duty

Confucius – Master K'ung

Confucius is traditionally considered to have been born in 551 BC, in the state of Lu during the Zhou dynasty, and to have died in 479 BC. His father died in Confucius' infancy and his mother raised him. He encountered severe constraints and poverty due to his life's situation. He seemed to have early success in his career as he obtained modest public offices within the bureaucracy that offered him positions of influence before he retired. Unfortunately, the Zhou dynasty was in serious decline during Confucius' time and the constant ebb and flow of the political situation served to disrupt his career and aspirations. His home state of Lu was lost to the empire when three influential and wealthy families joined together to wrest control of the state away from the center. Once his career as a mandarin bureaucrat stalled, Confucius lived as an itinerant teacher and bureaucrat in search of his next posting. During the Confucian era, bureaucrats could travel from state to state in search of employment. At one time, Confucius in desperation considered leaving China to seek service in barbarian countries. His difficulties and apparent frustration in gaining material success in his civilized homeland may have led to two traits in Confucian philosophy. First, and most importantly, he exhibited open disdain for personal gains or profits, something he argued that the true gentleman never sought; and second, he expressed dissatisfaction with civilized society and idealization of the 'Noble Savage'.

The Analects, in Chinese the *Lun Yu*, forms the primary body of his philosophy that has survived to the modern times. The English translation of *Lun Yu*, *Selected Sayings*, serves as the most accurate description of the masterpiece – basically a collection of sayings rather than a coherent text. The power of Confucian thought serves as much as a tribute to the discerning scholars who interpreted his sayings over the years as to Confucius' wisdom and understanding. Though many view his philosophy as lofty, Confucius addressed the practical aspects of day-to-day living almost exclusively. His great appeal today may stem from his being the most human of 'Great Officials', and the Great Official of all humanists.

owed to proper social conduct, or to following 'The Way' assumed dominance. Duty to the state that conflicted with duty to fathers and families became immoral and duty to the fathers and families prevailed ethically. Consequently, Confucius argued in Book 13, statement 18:

> The Duke of She addressed Master K'ung saying, In my country there was a man called Upright Kung. His father appropriated a sheep, and Kung bore witness against him. Master K'ung said, In my country the upright men are of quite another sort. A father will screen a son and a son his father – which incidentally does involve a sort of uprightness.

An old Chinese proverb reflects this important Confucian belief of moral duty and loyalty by stating, 'A man cannot be a good patriot and a good son'. This is an important factor as it begins to explain the concept of moral duty and loyalty, as Confucianism understands them. Though Confucian ethical and moral standards are rightfully held in high esteem by many Westerners who abhor the relativist nature of many Western philosophical schools, Confucianism is, in fact, a contextual philosophy which in some of its effects, resembles relativism.

According to the Confucians, mankind's other primary duty involved maintaining proper places and behaviors in society. This view did not translate to a prohibition against personal advancement or a demand for a static society. Confucians believed that men should strive to advance themselves as much as possible, so long as they maintained all the proper ritual behaviors for each stage of their lives' progression. Confucius viewed the strictures and requirements of The Way as the governor of all the gentlemen's actions. In Book 8, Chapter 13 of *The Analects*, Confucius elaborates on the strictures of the Confucian code by stating:

> The Master said, Be of unwavering good faith, love learning, if attacked, be ready to die for the good way. Do not enter a state that pursues dangerous courses, nor stay in one where the people have rebelled. When the Way prevails under Heaven, then show yourself; when it does not prevail, then hide …

As the above quote indicates, Confucius did not consider patriotism a virtue. 'My country, right or wrong!' certainly did not constitute the gentlemen's battle cry. The gentlemen vowed loyalty not to their country but to the Way. When a prince pursued 'dangerous courses' (or policies obstructing the proper observance of the Way or the maintenance of social order), Confucius recommended that the gentlemen desert their posts and leave for better-run states – advice that Confucius followed more than once! Consequently, many new Asian Emperors, indoctrinated in the Confucian way do not expect loyalty and demand constant reassurance of it from their employees. Canning K. N. Fok who worked as managing director of Hutchinson received a 1995 pay package of US$3.4 million – among the highest salaries in Hong Kong for professional managers. Yet, this pay came with certain demands from his boss Li Kai Shang. A former employee stated: 'If you work for Li you have got to keep showing your loyalty all the time.'

According to Confucian economic and social theory, a key part of good rule involved supplying a sufficient degree of wealth to all small men so that they can provide themselves and their families with basic necessities. This perspective, combined with the Confucian distaste for the profit motive and Taoist economic philosophy discussed earlier, lays the foundation for traditional Chinese economic principles followed by rulers for centuries. Unlike Western economic philosophy, Chinese traditional economics pursues the maintenance of minimally acceptable subsistence levels, not wealth, for all small men. The excess over and above subsistence level provided earned benefits for the greater men of society who provided good rule. Chapter 3 of Book 1 of the *Tao Te Ching*, elaborates this Taoist principle:

> Not to honor men of worth will keep the people from contention; not to value goods which are hard to come by will keep them from theft; not to display what is desirable will keep them from being unsettled of mind.

Chinese traditional economics suffocated the goal of wealth creation which meant displaying desirable goods, valuing rare goods, and in short, allowing greater wealth and concomitant honor to create 'contention among the people,' a situation good governments sought to prevent. Consequently, Confucian principles and traditional Chinese law forbade merchants from wearing fine clothes outside of their homes and riding horses or wagons. Merchants had to walk everywhere; thus the mandarins intended to show that merchants were no better than other small or lesser men.

The family

The family forms the overwhelming constant in Confucianism. The family dominates individuals' moral considerations and behaviors. The family sets the tone for individuals' relationships with others whom he meets daily; for individuals' relationships with sovereigns or other authority figures outside the family circles; and for individuals' relationships with society in general. Confucianism offers an immediate and unending perspective on the family: individuals owe responsibility to their nuclear and extended families, especially to their parents, and also to their ancestors. Consequently, the economic sufficiency mentioned above referred to sufficient income to house, clothe and feed living family members, and to make offerings and to conduct rituals for dead ancestors.

We have indicated above that the duty between a father and son superseded the duty between a man and his sovereign. In Confucian family ethics, a man's duty to his parents even exceeds his duty to his own person. The obedience and deference that a man owes his parents do not end on his gaining maturity; he owes his parents unflinching duty as a child, an adolescent, a grown man in his own dotage, and even after his parents' deaths. This, highly personal familial loyalty resounds in two chapters in *The Analects*. Book 4, Chapter 19 reads:

> The Master said, While father and mother are still alive, a good son does not wander far afield; or if he does so, goes only where he has said he was going.

And, Book 19, Chapter 18 reads:

> Master Tseng (a pupil of Confucius) said, I once heard the Master say, Filial piety such as that of Meng Chuang Tzu might in other respects be possible to imitate; but the way in which he changed neither his father's servants nor his father's domestic policy, that would indeed be hard to emulate.

The son need not have morally maintained his father's domestic policies and servants because of the concepts of personal loyalty in Chinese culture. The gentlemen owed loyalty to the Way and their prince, not to the state; and loyalty to the fathers constituted loyalty to the fathers' person and memory, not to the fathers' friends and subordinates. The reverse also holds true. The subordinates owe loyalty to their masters, not to their successors and heirs. Hence, Confucius' amazement stemmed from the son's continuing to maintain his father's servants, and also from the servants' continuing to owe loyalty to the heir. This concept of duty sheds light on Chinese business relationships' evolution over the centuries and in understanding some of the human resource practices and succession difficulties in many Chinese business enterprises today. Heirs sometimes do not feel the need to maintain continuity in the family businesses. Feuding after the patriarchs' deaths can assume vicious proportions leading to the companies' dissolutions. For example, Singapore food and beverage maker Yeo Hiap Seng slipped out of the founding Yeo family's control in 1994. This resulted from a bitter family feud in the wake of the death nine years earlier of the patriarch and founder Yeo Thian In.

The relationships and ethical behavior

The influential Chinese philosophical systems have historically stressed high ethical standards. Buddhism, much like Western ethical systems, focuses on the individuals' ethical duties and on the behaviors directly. For example, lying constitutes unethical behavior; ethical dilemmas arise when circumstances conjure costs to truthfulness, such as hurting loved ones' feelings.

The two systems of Chinese origin, Confucianism and Taoism, focus their ethical systems on those areas where dilemmas arise in Buddhist and Western ethics, in the area of relationships between people. Confucianism, with its constant focus on individuals' interactions within society, concentrates on five unidirectional relationships. The five relationships, from superior person to inferior person, occur from:

- Sovereign to Minister
- Father to Son
- Husband to Wife
- Older to Younger (some maintain it should be Older brother to Younger brother)
- Friendship

Mencius – The Second Sage

Mencius was born in the state of Lu in 372 BC and died in 289 BC. He served as Confucius' greatest adherent, and without him, our understanding of Confucius' philosophy would prove very different. Mencius did not just follow Confucius; he also contributed to Confucianism, including the prevalent Confucian view on human nature. Thus, he ensured that Confucianism would appear as a humanistic philosophy championing the inherent goodness of mankind. He introduced into Confucianism the concept that morality formed part of human nature as did base appetites. In direct opposition to Confucius' view, he argued that if a ruler ceased to govern for the people's benefit, the people had the right to rebel. In his own life, Confucius only influenced an elite group of educated courtiers. Mencius, more than anyone else, defeated the schools of philosophy that challenged Confucian principles of self-sacrifice, filial piety and duty. Yang Chu's philosophy of egoism seemed extremely attractive to some elements of society as it freed them of duty to sacrifice for society, or their families. Mo Tzu's universal love argument also proved attractive to many. China would have evolved as a less introspective and isolationist country had Mo's philosophy dominated, but it would also have de-emphasized duties to family, society, or proper behaviors. One must also wonder whether Mo's extreme pacifism could have survived the violence of the many invasions, both physical and spiritual (such as Britain's opium smuggling), which China suffered over the years. Without Mencius, Confucius's name and philosophy might have died a few decades after Confucius did.

Though Confucius would seem to owe Mencius a tremendous debt, Mencius' service, and the intertwining of their two names throughout history, seems fair. Mencius was born some 100 years after Confucius died, but their relationship began during Confucius' lifetime. Mencius' surname, Mang, and his birthplace in the state of Lu, indicate that his family was one of the three great families which usurped power in the state from the Zhou dynasty; their usurpation of power caused the collapse of Confucius' promising, early career within the local bureaucracy.

Taoism, which arose in China either slightly before or concurrently with Confucianism concentrates on six bidirectional relations. These relations appear more confining than those in Confucianism as they begin and end within the family. The six relations occur between:

- Father and Son
- Elder brother and Younger brother
- Husband and Wife

These Chinese ethical frameworks encapsulate all ethical duties; consequently, what ethical duties do individuals owe people falling outside these frameworks? Two traditional paths handle this dilemma in Confucianism. The first path argues that no true strangers exist. Some Confucians have argued that individuals have the duty to get to know unknown people with whom they interact, hence they no longer remain strangers but become friends. The second path applies the Taoist formulation of Elder brother/Younger brother, arguing that all men are brothers, and hence the relationship between strangers becomes one between Elder and Younger brothers. Regardless of whether the individuals recognize that all men are brothers and/or should be friends, the strangers will either be older or younger, and hence the duties of either elders to youngers, or youngers to elders will follow. Confucians argue that those following the Way will have no enemies – and so no ethical duties accrue to enemies.

The maintenance of social harmony constitutes another ethical duty within Confucianism. This requirement to maintain social harmony intrudes upon ethical concerns because someone treated unethically will resent that unethical treatment, and the resentment will result in social disharmony through efforts to obtain retribution or justice.

Confucianism entertains very high, but also contextual, some say situational, ethical standards. Westerners usually view situational ethics as employing flexible ethical standards for opportunistic benefits. Such negative connotations interfere with a true understanding of Confucian ethical standards. Confucian ethical standards, though contextual, are not situational. Confucian ethical standards do vary much more than do those within a single Western society or culture, but they actually possess much less flexibility. In Confucian societies, relationships determine the precise ethical behaviors and duties individuals owe each other; variations in duties have little to do with situations and everything to do with the contexts imposed by the relationships for which the standards abide. Hence, rather than one ethical standard, in Confucian societies as many as seven standards may exist – one standard for each of the five relationships. For those who cannot accept that all people fall into one of the five relationships but believe in maintaining social harmony, a sixth standard exists. Finally, for those who refuse to accept that all men fall within one of the five relationships, and recognize that not all people can adversely affect social harmony, a seventh standard exists. In all instances, particular situations have minimal effects on individuals' duties.

Little of Yang Chu's writings survive; most of his ethical philosophy comes to us through others' commentaries. Taoist principles greatly influenced Yang Chu's basically Confucian philosophies. One of Yang Chu's Taoist beliefs involved mankind's inherently evil nature. The two traditions disagreed on how to deal with this evil nature: while Yang Chu advocated extreme egoism, Taoism argued for the withdrawal of man from active participation in nature. Thus, scholars have generally represented Taoism as advocating high moral principles. In Taoism, however, outside forces imposed high moral principles on mankind. Mankind could only achieve high morality if thrust on them by forces external to their own nature. These forces included their own force of will, fear of punishment, and rationality, among others. One of Lao Tzu's duality paradoxes of Taoism logically concludes that if one wishes one's associates to treat one ethically, one should act unethically towards them. This conclusion follows from his verse in Chapter 18 of Book 1 of the *Tao Te Ching*:

When the great way falls into disuse
There are benevolence and rectitude;
When cleverness emerges
There is great hypocrisy;
When the six relations are at variance
There are filial children;
When the state is benighted
There are loyal ministers.

Differing ethical concepts

The West frowns upon, or ignores, many basic principles of business relations among Confucian societies such as the Overseas Chinese; the

Lao Tzu – His own ultimate duality paradox

Many believe that Lao Tzu was an older contemporary of Confucius. The name, 'Lao Tzu', actually means 'The Old Man'. Some believe he was a man named Li, a historian in charge of the Zhou dynasty's archives often called Tan the Historian. Others state that he was a man named Lao Lai Tzu, who was born in the same state, Ch'u, as Tan the Historian, and was a contemporary of both Confucius and Tan. Both men's historical biographies record a meeting between Confucius and Lao Tzu in which Lao Tzu bested Confucius. The meeting occurred when Confucius came to Lao Tzu for instruction in the rites. Depending upon whether a supporter of Confucius or a critic of his recounts the story, Confucius returns either showing respect for Lao Tzu's age and great wisdom, or admitting that Lao Tzu had an understanding far beyond his own. Traditionally, Lao Tzu retired from public life and was leaving to seek the contemplative life of a holy hermit, when the Keeper of the Pass out of the Zhou Empire's realm to the West asked Lao Tzu to write a book for him. Lao Tzu wrote the *Tao Te Ching*, in which he explains the meaning of the Way and virtuous behavior. Though he wrote it in 5000 Chinese characters, the *Tao Te Ching* today consists of some 5250 characters. It has become the most translated book of Chinese literature and philosophy. Lao Tzu then passed through the gates to his life of meditation and into history as one of the world's greatest philosophers. Lore has him living for at least 160 years, and some say for over 200 years.

Just as he would have intimated in one of his duality paradoxes, however, the harder historians try to establish his existence, the more evasive his physical essence becomes, and finally he simply disappears. Chinese historians record his meeting with Confucius taking place in 518 BC; yet, they also record his son as a general in the Principality of Wei's army in 273 BC. Also, many stories exist of meetings between Confucius and elder scholars who severely outclassed Confucius. Confucius' critics spread these stories over the years in order to undermine his philosophical credibility.

reverse also holds as the Overseas Chinese frown upon or ignore many basic principles of doing business in Western societies. Chinese scholar, Xiaotong Fei in his 1992 book, *From the Soil: The Foundation of Chinese Society*, made a civilizational argument for these differences between Western and Eastern societies; these arguments extend to their business societies. Fei argued that to compare Western and Eastern cultures, one must address both societies' foundations. Western societies draw on transcendental monotheism. Consequently, Western ethical concepts and perceptions of mankind's position in the world begin with mankind's relationship with God; they generally have universal prescriptions such as 'Thou shalt not lie'. Conversely, in many Eastern societies, such as those of the Overseas Chinese, the Heaven's constitute a given not discussed at length. Consequently, Eastern ethical concepts and perceptions of mankind's position in the world draw upon the relationships operating at the time; the relationships' dominance and direction stem from 'natural orders' – husband over wife, elder over younger, or sovereign over minister. In Eastern societies, one's humanity derives from proper role playing in that natural order, not from individuality as in the West.

In the Confucian ethical system that dominates Chinese culture, human relationships, with the foundation of the family, prescribe appropriate behaviors and standards. Behaviors clearly specified within Confucian thought demand rigid conformity to preserve morality and little flexibility exists. The behaviors have to synchronize with clearly specified rites that often cover detailed contexts and include minutiae such as the proper lengths for garment sleeves (right and left sleeves had to be of different lengths). On the other hand, virtually any behaviors outside contexts covered by Confucian thought that do not cause significant social disharmony prove acceptable and moral. Importantly, because of Chinese relationships' extremely personal natures, personal relationships must exist for ethical duties to exist.

Additionally, Western systems of thought establish different relational norms and practices for non-family relationships, and especially for business relationships. In Confucian societies, business relations basically extend family relations. This ethical difference has had dramatic effects on many aspects of cross-national business. Because all relationships extend familial relationships, behaviors only deemed acceptable within families in Western nations, such as accepting a business partner's word as collateral, can assume accepted practice in Chinese business relationships.

In recent decades, as Asian markets, economies and trade have become increasingly important, Western multinationals and local Asian businesses have reported greater numbers of ethical conflicts and misunderstandings, especially involving the sanctity of signed contracts and intellectual property rights. These misunderstandings may stem from differing ethical concepts. For example, Acer Computers had to establish an office in the United States to monitor its own technological activities and to issue warnings when Acer's worldwide operations appeared about to violate intellectual property rights. Acer's Taiwanese management at its headquarters often failed to realize when they may inadvertently violate property rights. We will discuss similar misunderstandings, and methods to circumvent them, in some of the forthcoming chapters.

Chapter Three

The Overseas Chinese Today:

not the family business, but the family as a business

'When I was asked by a friend if I would consider managing a family controlled corporation, my reaction was, "You must be joking." '

Mr Koh Boon Hwee, former managing director, Hewlett-Packard, Singapore, now executive chairman, Wuthelam Group

Introduction

Western academics, media and managers have increased scrutiny of Asian business practices as different Asian economies have assumed importance for global trade and markets; yet, lack of systematic information and a coherent theory of the regional business culture often limit their gaining a true comprehension of business practices in the region. Drawing on our research and experiences with regional companies, and our grasp of the region's historical and cultural roots, we will develop an understanding of the business environments of the Overseas Chinese networks that dominate Southeast Asian economies and increasingly compete with multinational corporations from the West, Japan and Korea. In this, the third and last of our foundation chapters, we will trace the Overseas Chinese philosophical and cultural roots into their present-day business environments to paint a fuller picture of the New Asian Emperors as a people and as a business force.

First, we describe some general characteristics of Chinese networks. Next we elaborate on the historical and environmental circumstances that shaped the Overseas Chinese networks. Finally, we describe some cultural characteristics that distinguish the Overseas Chinese from other major Asian competitors, the Japanese.

What is a Chinese network?

Xiaotong Fei (1992) identified five distinctive general characteristics of Chinese networks. These characteristics include:

- Chinese networks are discontinuous.
- Chinese networks have hierarchical and dyadic ties.
- Chinese networks emphasize uprightness.
- Chinese networks view morality as contextual.
- Chinese networks have flexible boundaries that change with circumstances.

Discontinuity

Unlike Westerners, the Chinese do not distinguish between work-related, family-related and socially related networks; for them, all of these fuse together. As we mentioned in Chapter One, the Overseas Chinese networks have five bases: clan, language, location, guild, and trust. The Overseas Chinese participate in more than one type of network, and membership in one does not guarantee membership in another. For example, one can serve as a member of a clan-based network, a locality-based network, a linguistically-based network, and possibly a guild-based network, and each network will usually, though not always, have independence from others. Additionally, guild-based networks have regional specifications.

Individuals enjoy unique duties, responsibilities and authorities within networks and across networks empowering them differently to take action on behalf their businesses. In an Overseas Chinese business network or company, individuals with similar titles may exercise drastically different levels of authority and responsibility – and their stature may vary across networks affecting their overall power.

Consequently, Overseas Chinese businessmen seeking partners can choose from several different networks – though they must do so with care. An ally within one network may oppose projects or business partners in another as interests may clash. Generally, though, Chinese businessmen avoid generating opposition and work on creating support.

Hierarchical and dyadic ties

Relationships within networks approximate dyadic and directional relations within Confucian families (described in the previous chapter); the relationships' superior members define the relationships. Individuals have direct relationships with all the networks' members. The persons with higher statures within these networks' dyads have the upper hands within the relationship. Respect within networks is often derived from one's ability to move flawlessly from dominant roles to subordinate roles and back to dominant roles within the networks – depending on one's positions relative to the different people interacted with in business and social activities. The required duties, responsibilities and behaviors can vary significantly based upon relative positions within networks. Individuals' relative positions can also vary through recent performance, especially among younger members trying to establish themselves. Thus, keeping track of everyone's relative position, especially in a large network, may prove monumental. Unlike younger members, older members generally enjoy more stability as they automatically retain rank and prestige through age and seniority.

Foreign managers when doing business with the Overseas Chinese should garner as much information as possible on the individuals they deal with regularly, occasionally, and plan to deal with in the future. Relative positions of both the Overseas Chinese and the foreign managers mold expectations. Also, foreign managers should

> ### The Federation of Hokkien Associations of Malaysia – A traditional dialect network
>
> The Federation of Hokkien Associations of Malaysia forms Malaysia's pre-eminent dialect federation. It serves as the peak body of Hokkien associations in Malaysia and some of Malaysia's most prominent businessmen serve or have served on its executive committee – including Lim Goh Tong, head of the Genting Group; Tiong Hiew King, controller of the Rimbunan Hijau timber and logging company and the late Loh Boon Siew, controller of the Boon Siew Group. The federation has 138 affiliated associations. Most of the members have relatively traditional outlooks and tend to have Chinese educations. Despite its Hokkien membership, the federation conducts business in Mandarin as many Hokkien subdialects are mutually unintelligible.
>
> The federation, active in business, formed Hoklian Holdings, its business arm, almost two decades ago. Apart from its Malaysian investments, the company recently agreed with Anxi subprovince in Fujian, China to build a hotel and is also engaging in other investments there. Anxi forms the ancestral region for several senior federation executives. The federation receives regular visits from Anxi business delegations.
>
> The federation actively engages in exchanges and conducts international meetings with other Hokkien associations worldwide.

remember that older members of Chinese business organizations often enjoy significantly greater power and influence than their official titles may indicate.

Uprightness

Uprightness involves the ability and willingness to perform all the expected behaviors at the appropriate times and in the appropriate fashions. In the West, trust arises when people gain reputations for doing what they said they would do. In the Chinese sense, trust has two elements: the first involves the same concept of trust as that the West employs; the second involves uprightness. Uprightness constitutes an important behavioral ideal, and without it, complete trust in the Chinese sense cannot exist.

Western managers failing to perform expected behaviors encounter problems when dealing with Overseas Chinese businessmen. The Overseas Chinese perceive the Westerner as not upright and withdraw accordingly. Conversely, the Western managers, who may have acted in good faith, see their business relationships disintegrate, and usually press harder for closure. In many Southeast and East Asian countries dominated by the Overseas Chinese, Western managers may initially invest in good guides for help through the formalities. Good guides may aid in preserving upright behaviors until the Western managers have gained experience and established local reputations. Because of the emphasis on personal relationships, the Western managers' local reputations will establish the degrees of trust and loyalty extended to their companies by the networks – even for companies active in Asia for decades.

Contextual morality

As we discussed in detail in Chapter Two, among the Overseas Chinese, ethical standards vary with business relationships. Longer and better-established relationships with equals or superiors entail higher standards than shorter, fleeting relationships with inferiors.

Western companies should also remember relationships' personal natures among the Overseas Chinese. Many Western companies rotate executives through Asian subsidiaries and offices. However, their incoming executives do not automatically inherit the outgoing executives' goodwill and strong relationships, or indeed their opponents. Companies do not own franchises of trust and uprightness in Asia – individuals do.

Flexible boundaries

Among the Overseas Chinese, the networks' boundaries have flexibility and vary with circumstances much more than they do among Western networks. Chinese networks exhibit very personal, though relatively low-strength, ties of loyalty. Individuals' personal networks expand and contract with their relative successes (as personal contacts do for Westerners); individuals' networks for business projects vary with partners, locality and the projects' natures. A plethora of circumstantial factors (too many to enumerate) may affect the precise make-up of any individual's business network in any one instance.

Consequently, Western managers have difficulties judging who to contact, or how much to divulge to potential partners. Also, the wrong choice of partners (for example one viewed as untrustworthy or not upright) can cause a company difficulties for extended periods of time.

Historical and environmental effects on the Overseas Chinese business networks

Many Overseas Chinese, especially those in Hong Kong and Taiwan, started as merchants and traders. Trading formed the predominant business for the merchant class families in China. These Overseas Chinese left China as factors and representatives for prosperous traders, usually blood relations from their home districts. Other

---

The world Chinese business network –
tribal network for the information age

In 1995, the Singapore Chinese Chamber of Commerce and Industry (SCCCI) formally launched on the Internet what it called a new tribal network – The World Chinese Business Network (WCBN). With connections to Chinese Chambers of Commerce worldwide, the WCBN provides a computer network to link ethnic Chinese executives all over the world and a massive database containing information on businesses run by the Overseas Chinese. The SCCCI said, 'The WCBN is aimed at strengthening the networking of Chinese businessmen throughout the world. It is designed to help Chinese businessmen worldwide in establishing contacts and exchanging information with one another in a speedy and systematic manner.' Singaporean minister for information and the arts, Brigadier General (BG) George Yeo, said that tribal networks will become very important in the future, 'a lot of business will be done over these networks.'

WCBN, a brainchild of senior minister Lee Kuan Yew, constitutes the first online link among Chinese traders worldwide. In 1993, senior minister Lee at the Second World Chinese Entrepreneurs Convention proposed that the networking of the Overseas Chinese be made efficient by providing relevant data on the Internet. With the technical assistance of the Institute of Systems Science and Netcenter (Singapore) and a financial grant of US$100,000 from Singapore's National Science and Technology Board, the SCCCI then proceeded to undertake the US$500,000 project. The WCBN provides detailed corporate information on over 15,000 Overseas Chinese companies from over fifteen countries on subsidiaries, products, marketing and distribution operations. Information is accessible by punching in key words and is available in both English and Chinese. However, BG Yeo was quick to point that that such business networks could only provide 'public domains' for the transfer of information: companies would have to move into the 'private domain' to strike deals. 'In the corporate world, those who can make more money are those who have more information than others. We all know that while some information can be made freely available, some must be kept confidential', BG Yeo said.

The WCBN may be accessed on the Internet at the following URL: http://www.cbn.com.sg and the service is currently provided free of charge.

Overseas Chinese, especially those in Southeast Asia, left China as coolies to work for Chinese and European traders, plantation owners, governments and semi-governmental authorities. They worked hard, lived extremely frugally and saved money until they could strike out on their own (Chan and Chiang, 1994). Once these Overseas Chinese gained some degree of prosperity, they often moved into property-related businesses, and then into any business deemed profitable.

Table 3.1 presents a small sample of Overseas Chinese families and the businesses in which they operate. The founders of the Overseas Chinese companies, though highly intelligent, generally had little formal education and even less formal, Western-style business education. Generally, these patriarchs resembled generations of Western businessmen before the founding of the great and not-so-great Western business schools. However, significant factors distinguished the Overseas Chinese patriarchs' upbringing and training and differentiated them from their Western counterparts.

The business education of the founders of today's major Overseas Chinese companies originated from their experiences and their training in their Confucian village schools. The expansion of their businesses followed the dictates of their education, their culture and their experiences. Their education and culture possessed the Confucian emphasis on the family, and employed the Confucian perspective of societal relationships as extensions of, yet subordinate to, familial relationships.

The experiences of the Overseas Chinese companies' patriarchs in China and their new homelands reinforced their Confucian perspective of relying only on families or on select networks. Back in China, the philosophers had traditionally considered merchants as the lowest class of humanity; the government had persecuted merchants for their mobility, and especially so when that mobility involved contacts with foreigners. In their new overseas homes, the local governments and people often admired the Overseas Chinese business skills; but as communities of outsiders without their home country government's protection, the Overseas Chinese provided convenient scapegoats for colonial and local governments to blame for policy mistakes and disasters. In Batavia, 10,000 Overseas Chinese were massacred. In the Spanish colony of the Philippines, non-Catholic Chinese were periodically persecuted, and occasionally massacred; in one such event about 25,000 Chinese were massacred in the Manila-based Chinese community alone. British colonial governors also frequently encouraged feuds between the Overseas Chinese secret societies: these governors provoked local internal conflicts and withheld peacekeeping troops until they felt sufficient numbers of Overseas Chinese had been killed (Wang, 1991; Fernandez-Armesto, 1995).

Table 3.1 Some families and businesses in the Overseas Chinese business networks

Family/Leader   *Primary businesses*

Indonesia

Liem Sioe Liong   Cement, processed foods, flour milling, steel, banking, real estate, and investments

Eka Tjipta Widjaja   Diversified investments
Mochtar Riaddy   Property, banking, and insurance
Suhargo Gondokusumo   Agri-industries and property
Prajogo Pangestu   Timber and car assembly

Malaysia

Robert Kuok   Plantations, sugar and wood processing, media, and hotels

Quek Leng Chan   Finance and diversified investments
Lim Goh Tong   Casinos and real estate
Vincent Tan   Leisure, manufacturing, and investment

Philippines

Lucio Tan   Beer, tobacco, banking, and investment
Henry Sy   Retailing, cement, and investment
Alfonso Yuchengco   Banking and insurance
Antonio Cojuangco   Telecommunications and real estate
John Gokongwei   Real estate and diversified investments

Thailand

Chearavanont Family   Agri-business, real estate, and telecommunications

Kanjanapas Family   Real estate, transport, and finance
Ratanarak Family   Cement, banking, and telecommunications

Sophonpanich Family   Banking, real estate, and investments
Lamsam Family   Banking and real estate

Table 3.1   (*continued*)

Family/Leader	Primary businesses
Hong Kong*	
Kuok Family	Real estate, banking, and infrastructural developments
Lee Shau-Kee	Real estate, fuel, transportation, hotels, and resorts
Li Kai Shang	Real estate, construction, infrastructural developments, and utilities
Pao Family	Real estate, cable television, infrastructural developments, and transportation
Singapore	
Kwek Leng Beng	Real estate, hotels, and financial services
Ng Teng Fong	Real estate, hotels, food and beverages
Khoo Teck Puat	Hotels and real estate
Wee Cho Yaw	Banking, real estate, and hotels
Lee Seng Wee	Banking, plantations, insurance, brewing, and trading
Goh Cheng Liang	Paint, hotels, retailing, and real estate
Oei Hong Leong	Beer, tires, and consumer products
Macao	
Stanley Ho	Real estate and casinos
Taiwan	
Stan Shih	Computers
Tsai Wan Lin	Insurance, real estate, and construction
Wang Yung Chin	Petrochemicals and diversified manufacturing
Wu Tung Chin	Real estate, insurance, banking, retailing, and diversified manufacturing
Hsu Yu Ziang	Textiles, retailing, cement, and conglomerate diversification
Koo Chen Fu	Banking, cement, and diversified financial services

* Hong Kong is now a special administrative region of the People's Republic of China.

The Indonesian family conglomerates –
one for all and all for one

The Overseas Chinese control more than 33 major conglomerates in Indonesia and almost all of them are interlinked. In recent years, interlinkages occurred through cross-shareholdings and directorships, joint ventures between conglomerates and family links such as marriages between the major business families. Overseas Chinese controlled conglomerates linked by family connections include the Lippo Group and the Myapada Group; the Lippo Group and Panin Bank; the Gadjah Tunggal Group and the Ometraco Group; the Gunung Sewu Group and the Dharmala Group; and, the Gemala Group and the Danamon Group.

The interlinkages have turned potential competitors into colleagues, allowing the conglomerates to access new sources of capital and to maintain market share. The management of political risk forms one important byproduct of the interlinkages. If the Indonesian government, in the form of one of ex-President Suharto's successors, turns unfavorable towards even one conglomerate, the interlinkages ensure that the unfavorable currents will flow onto most of the other major conglomerates. Consequently, each conglomerate has a vested interest in maintaining all the others' interests. Future political leaders will probably not challenge the conglomerates' economic positions for fear of widespread economic repercussions. The conglomerates have responded to political uncertainty in Indonesia by arraying themselves as interdependent dominos.

Some conglomerates also have links to key members of the Suharto family, particularly to ex-President Suharto's sons and daughters through joint ventures. Although well-connected *pribumi* or ethnic Indonesian politicians bring small amounts of equity to the joint ventures, they achieve a high proportion of the profits: the *pribumis* generally bring political capital; by negotiating bureaucratic and regulatory obstacles, they earn high returns on their political capital.

These circumstances created a people fiercely loyal to their families and network partners, and dependent on one another rather than any governing authorities. The Overseas Chinese also displayed pronounced preferences for maintaining significant proportions of their wealth in liquid forms and for physically dispersed rather than concentrated fixed investments. Liquid assets proved convenient in forced flight, and physically dispersed investments provided geographical diversity, hedging risks in anti-Chinese attacks.

Physically dispersed fixed assets also reinforced the networks among family businesses. The Overseas Chinese only trusted close associates; and local on-site managers had to have extensive independent authority to disburse assets quickly in slow communications systems and perilous times. Increased diversification of the Overseas Chinese assets, and their growing physical dispersion, hindered constant surveillance and guidance from the family businesses' head. Consequently, purely trust-based relations emerged as potent forces in the networks.

Despite their great fortunes, most of the New Asian Emperors maintained relatively small companies. The small companies precluded confiscation or destruction of any one company from seriously affecting overall financial positions. Second, without primogeniture and with the normal emphasis on large families that most traditional cultures have, the Overseas Chinese envisioned their companies dissolving after the patriarchs' deaths. Dissecting larger companies would create greater economic dislocation for the families than distributing bunches of smaller, unrelated companies. Consequently, Overseas Chinese companies rarely achieved scale or scope economies to become effective international competitors; those that did achieve large size often came crashing down after their founders' deaths. The best of the New Asian Emperors, such as Li Kai Shang of Hong Kong, have smaller families, and practice primogeniture so that single sons, usually the eldest, inherit the greater parts of their estates.

The Confucian emphasis on personal relationships, with the historical lack of institutional support from government agencies, reinforced the Overseas Chinese emphasis on personal relationships. These combined factors also ensured that the families and their businesses never separated. Though many Overseas Chinese companies form legal corporations, and the family bases of some companies appear weak, most families still control their companies either outright or through their networks' partners with whom the families share projects and interlocking directorates.

As Table 3.1 shows, the Overseas Chinese have generally not focused on primary businesses, often displaying extreme conglomerate diversification. Other business networks in developing countries such as the Overseas Indian networks and Latin American *grupos* also display unrelated conglomerate diversification (Haley and Haley, 1997, 1998). And, in the last century, as the United States industrialized, many American companies engaged in unrelated diversification (Heilbroner and Singer, 1984). Yet, the Overseas Chinese appear to have taken unrelated conglomerate diversification to a new level. With New Asian Emperor Robert Kuok, one becomes hard pressed to find a business in which he does not engage – food, luxury and middle-market hotels, real estate, sugar and oil palm plantations, newspapers – including the world's most profitable newspaper, the *South China Morning Post*. He has large investments in Indonesia, Hong Kong, China, Australia, Malaysia, Singapore, the Philippines and Thailand. He owns a piece of Citic-Pacific, the Beijing-controlled conglomerate. His acumen provides the only glue for his diverse business interests; as Kuok describes his role, 'I am the little string that ties the rings together'.

The Overseas Chinese generally comprised an independent lot. Faced with harsh economic realities and experiences that contradicted their cultural teachings, they rebelled. Their culture advised marginal acceptability of the profit motive; their governments advocated accepting their inferior lots in life. Yet, they rejected cultural arguments and governmental restrictions and fought for their families' livelihoods. In a culture emphasizing conformity, they refused to conform. This refusal to conform, of course, constituted a uniquely Confucian rebellion – that of a group's refusal to conform rather than any individual's refusal. The groups within their memberships required the same degrees of conservative conformity as the societies against which they were rebelling; the groups rebelled because the dominant groups, or networks, or members did.

We have discussed some powerful influences on the Overseas Chinese; however, throughout their history, these hardy people have encountered diverse influences which have honed their intellectual agility and enhanced their adaptability. Most of the New Asian Emperors have faced human nature and confronted harsh economic realities; and, most have lived under colonial and non-colonial governments with legal systems completely foreign to Confucian minds. In Southeast Asia, only Thailand eluded colonial rule. Hong

Robert Kuok – network Zen master

If anyone were proclaimed a Zen master of networking, it would be Malaysian-born, Singapore-educated Robert Kuok. His skill at managing within the network's structure has earned him the sobriquet of the 'World's shrewdest businessman' from *Forbes* magazine. Just as many other prominent Overseas Chinese businessmen, Kuok has substantial operations in several countries. Pinpointing some of his companies' headquarters can often prove confusing. Sometimes a company's operations become so closely associated with a host country that each subsidiary appears local. The Far East Group, headed by tycoon Ng Teng Fong, provides such an example. The Far East Group has substantial stakes in both Hong Kong and Singapore, and in both instances, Far East in Singapore, and Sinoland in Hong Kong, the operations seem local.

With other companies, situations may arise similar to the Kuok Group's and any company's headquarters may become mobile. Singapore served as Kuok's first headquarters because of the company's early emphasis on trading and Singapore's position as an entrepot. Singapore's position as headquarters was further enhanced after he founded his phenomenally successful Shang-ri-La Hotel chain with its flagship hotel in Singapore. However, later, according to rumors, Kuok moved his headquarters to Malaysia due to differences with the local authorities, and many still consider Kuok a Malaysian businessman. He has vast holdings in properties, plantations, utilities and dozens of other businesses in Malaysia. In the 1970s he earned the title of the 'Sugar King' because he controlled 10 per cent of the world's sugar trade. Regardless, Hong Kong hosts his headquarters these days; different members of his family steer various businesses in different countries. Though Hong Kong plays official host to the Kuok Group's headquarters, operationally, the other nodes in Kuok's network web can equal the headquarters in importance, and sometimes surpass it.

Seemingly proving the Confucian reasons for bias against merchants, Kuok has demonstrated extreme mobility, moving headquarters from one location and state to another. Sometimes he moves for convenience, sometimes for political reasons, and sometimes for strategic preferences. Mostly, the network Zen master doesn't care to explain his reasons.

Kong only reverted to Chinese control in 1997; Macao, Portugal's colony next to Hong Kong, will revert to Chinese control in 1999. Consequently, Robert Kuok could say, 'I adapt like a chameleon to the particular society where I am operating at the moment.' Robert Riley, managing director of Mandarin Oriental Hotel Group and a fierce competitor of Kuok said, 'He's a local everywhere he goes.'

Western managers should remember that the Overseas Chinese managers, unlike their counterparts in Korea and Japan, have tremendous capabilities for radical action. Because of most companies' authoritarian natures, individuals with sufficient stature can make and implement decisions blazingly fast. We will now conclude this chapter by comparing the Overseas Chinese business culture with that of the Japanese.

Distinguishing cultural traits

Several authors have argued that Asia will follow Japan's technological trajectory in a flying-geese formation (Yamashita, 1991). Nakamura (1992) extended this flying-geese, Japan-dominated perspective of Asian development to strategic management by arguing that strategic decision-making in Asia was evolving as it did in Japan: the developing Asian countries were following Japan as flying geese follow a leader. Although certain similarities exist between the Japanese economy's evolution and those of the Asian nations, significant economic and cultural differences indicate flaws in Nakamura's (1992) arguments. This section elaborates on the region-specific characteristics that differentiate the Overseas Chinese culture from their Japanese competitors' culture.

Like the Japanese, most Asian economies constitute managed economies that have depended primarily on export-led growth; however, key differences lie in the sources and directions of their exports. Japanese companies have always formed Japan's principal sources of exports and until recently, Japanese exports focused on North America and Europe. Among those economies dominated by the Overseas Chinese, manufacturing-based multinational corporations have formed the principal sources of exports to Western nations; the Overseas Chinese and other local companies have primarily concentrated on the local markets that Western companies now perceive as so important (Haley and Tan, 1996; Haley and Haley, 1997, 1998). As we establish in the subsequent chapter, local, Asian markets constitute an informational void for market-related information upon which so many corporate decisions depend in the West (Haley and Tan, 1996, 1998). Overseas Chinese companies have grown and developed their management decision-making and management systems primarily in competition with one another in this information-scarce environment, rather than in competition with Western multinational corporations and Western domestic companies in economically mature, information-rich environments. Consequently, the economic similarities between Japan and its Asian neighbors assume less significance. Table 3.2 (Haley and Haley, 1997, 1998) summarizes some significant cultural differences between

Table 3.2 Cultural similarities and differences between the Chinese and Japanese

Attributes	Chinese	Japanese
Firm		
Merchants	Reviled	Exalted
Primogeniture	None	Strong
Company's life span	Short	Long
Loyalty		
Family definition	Blood	Role
Focus	Individual	Institution
Intensity	Low	High
Filial piety vs. patriotism	Opposed	Equivalent
Commercial trust		
Ethical foundation	Five relationships and social harmony	Mutual self-interest
Ethical focus	The Way	Service to father figure
Expectations of benefits	Immediate and up-front	Long-term and delayed

the Chinese and Japanese. These cultural differences have influenced the Overseas Chinese networks' companies, their concepts of loyalty as well as the bases for commercial trust and decision-making in business dealings – just as the Japanese culture and competitive environments have affected Japanese companies on these issues.

Firm-related attributes

Merchants – The Japanese and Chinese cultures have exhibited opposing attitudes towards merchants. The Japanese culture incorporates an economic philosophy of growth that exalts merchants. The Confucian culture of the Overseas Chinese, however, exalts peasants and reviles and persecutes merchants. As noted in the previous chapter, Confucian philosophers frowned upon merchants whom they perceived as excessively concerned with profits rather than 'The Way' (Lau, 1995; Legge, 1970; Waley, 1996); the philosophers also saw merchants as mobile, and thus unreliable supporters of rulers. Not surprisingly, innumerable waves of Overseas Chinese flooded South and Southeast Asia over the centuries: every wave corresponded to a period of persecution against the merchants.

Primogeniture and companies' life spans – Another difference between Chinese and Japanese customs revolves around primogeniture. These customs have influenced companies' life spans. Confucian customs emphasize large families and ban primogeniture; consequently, the ancient Chinese saying, 'No fortune survives the third generation'. Most of today's major Overseas Chinese companies have survived only as far as the second generation of managers (Chu and MacMurray, 1993). Japanese customs, on the other hand, have always emphasized primogeniture, although according to custom the oldest son need not necessarily inherit. Consequently, wealthy Japanese families have often bequeathed family fortunes to their most capable sons to build concentrated and continued wealth. Japanese companies, such as Mitsubishi, have survived for a considerable time in some form. Indeed, some of Japan's major companies began centuries ago as family companies that evolved through growth, and the military establishment's encouragement in the late nineteenth and early twentieth centuries, into the Japanese *keiretsu* conglomerates of today.

Loyalty-related attributes

Family, focus and intensity – In Japanese culture, loyalties, though very strong, have functional bases: family members owe filial loyalties to the breadwinners, not to the actual fathers. Conversely, in Chinese culture, family members owe filial loyalties to the fathers, regardless of who actually serves as the breadwinners in the families; members of the Overseas Chinese networks share highly personalized, as opposed to functional, bases for loyalties. In the Chinese culture, loyalties accrue to individuals; members often do not transfer loyalties to friends or employers and hence employees' loyalties frequently do not survive individual managers or transfer to companies.

Patriotism – The relationships that the Japanese and Chinese perceive between individuals and societies also differ. These associations affect the ways in which the Overseas Chinese contribute to their adopted and native countries. A Japanese adage posits that: 'To be a good patriot is to be a good son'. Alternatively, the equivalent adage in China argues that 'One cannot be both a good patriot and a good son'. Hence, Japanese employees demonstrate intense loyalty for their father figures, their employers, who by extension, serve as the emperor's symbolic representatives. Conversely, Overseas Chinese employees demonstrate relatively weak loyalties to employers, unless they work for their families' companies or have been incorporated into the extended business families.

Trust-related attributes

Ethical foundations – Concepts of ethics differ significantly between the two cultures (Haley, G. T., 1997b; Haley and Haley, 1997, 1998) affecting the bases of commercial trust. In the Japanese view, contractual duties bind and familial and friendship ties help, but ties of personal and corporate mutual self-interest prove paramount; trust in commercial relationships derives from perceived, mutual self-interest. Hence, the numerous social gatherings in which potential business associates seek out similarities in outlooks, perspectives and values.

As elaborated in the previous chapter, among the Overseas Chinese, five relationships define ethical duty:

1 Sovereign and Minister
2 Father and Son
3 Husband and Wife
4 Elder brother and Younger brother
5 Friends.

If relationships fall outside the above categories, then the primary ethical duty involves maintaining social harmony. Specific, contextual relationship-based, normative ethical duties and expected behaviors regulate relationships, not the universal constants. Thus, without familial or established friendship ties, trust rarely exists in commercial relationships with the Overseas Chinese. To work well with them, foreign business associates must build non-commercial ties of friendship or family. Outside of established relationships, the Overseas Chinese, unconstrained by Western ethical concepts of level playing fields, prove brutal competitors. Confucian societies accept steeply hierarchical structures and inherent inequalities of men's aptitudes and stations in life as necessary conditions for social good. Hence, Indonesian Chinese bankers can ethically forward strangers' loan applications as strategically important information to members of their business networks doing business in the same area and industry as the loan applicant. Strangers, in some interpretations of Confucian ethics, do not fall within the Confucian contextual framework of Confucian ethics and often cannot disrupt social harmony in their disappointment and anger.

Ethical focus – The two cultures' ethics demonstrate different normative focal points. The Overseas Chinese, influenced by Confucian philosophies, believe individuals should behave appropriately to their stations within the dyadic framework of their relationships and in accordance with 'The Way'. The Chinese employers may often seem like emperors as businesses serve as extensions of families and fathers enjoy pre-eminent positions. To the Japanese, individuals should serve their superiors (their father figures), and through their superiors, patriotically, their emperors. Their loyalties to their companies originate from their employers symbolically representing their emperor, rather than from their companies representing an extension of their families.

Expectations of benefits – The Overseas Chinese differ from the Japanese in their expectations of benefits from contractual relationships. The Overseas Chinese will enter or maintain contractual relationships only if they receive minimal benefits and have the expectations of making profits within a relatively short period of time when compared with Japanese firms: when the benefits and expectations fade, so do contractual duties for the most part. The Overseas Chinese will invest time, money and effort, but they expect to see tangible benefits up-front (Redding, 1996). The Overseas Chinese, whose history includes many episodes of persecution in Southeast Asia, also exhibit a hard-edged negotiating style and expect benefits that match the efforts they invest in projects (Redding, 1996). Signed contracts may often begin, rather than end, negotiations (Haley and Tan, 1996); consequently, commercial partners should expect some quibbling over the contracts' terms. Because of their experiences with foreign populations, the Overseas Chinese, unlike the Japanese, desire tangible returns and often maintain substantial holdings of liquid assets (Haley, G. T., 1997a).

This section has demonstrated the significant cultural differences that exist between the Chinese and Japanese cultures which relate to their business practices. These differences strongly suggest that despite Nakamura's (1992) claim, strategic management of the Overseas Chinese differs significantly from that of Japanese companies, and is likely to continue to do so.

In our next chapter, we will discuss the strategic planning environment that exists in Southeast Asia. We will speculate on why it exists and present the unique strategic planning and decision-making system that the Overseas Chinese have developed to take advantage of their special environment, the informational void.

Part Two

The Foundations of Analysis

Chapter Four

Introduction to an Informational Void:

the black hole of Southeast Asia

'In Chinese business circles, the emphasis is on harmony. People agree to compete or not to compete.'

Cheung Kim Hung, editor-in-chief, *Next Magazine*, Hong Kong

Introduction

Most managers and researchers acknowledge that emerging and newly industrialized markets do not have the same quantity and quality of secondary data as markets in the long-industrialized North American and Western European economies. In this chapter we will discuss this informational void with respect to Southeast Asia. We discuss the reasons for this informational void and the strategies which the Overseas Chinese regional managers use to cope with, and adapt to it. We also delineate how regional managers remain current with the region's fast-changing business, cultural and competitive environments. In both instances, the unique, highly intuitive style of strategic management which they have developed and mastered provides the key to their competitive advantages.

An old adage posits that the quality of one's decisions depends upon the quality of one's information. The more complex the situation, the more important to have the appropriate data to analyze. The information generated through analyses provides the necessary understanding of the situation to make optimal decisions. Yet, managers conducting strategic planning in the prescribed manners in Southeast Asia's complex environments will never have sufficient data to justify taking action. Southeast Asia represents an informational black hole. This situation exists regardless of the increasingly important role that Southeast Asia is playing in the world economy.

Despite last year's economic shocks, Southeast Asia constitutes a very special market. Over a 30-year period, no economic region in history has grown faster. Unlike Japan and South Korea, which also used export-led growth to spur economic development, Southeast Asia maintains among the freest markets in the world. Consequently, though Southeast Asian exports have grown significantly over the years, so have its imports. These imports surged when the regional economies embarked on restructuring and value-added manufacturing. Indeed from 1993–98, Southeast Asia constituted the only economic region outside of North America that served as a net importer of goods. The region's growth provided jobs and economic growth for other regions of the world.

Foreign multinational corporations primarily conduct Southeast Asia's trade with the Western industrialized economies. The region's own companies, including those of the New Asian Emperors, have mainly emphasized a regional thrust to their developmental and trade ties. At first, the regional companies' small sizes hindered their efforts in international competition. In recent years, the region's growth and market opportunities have attracted the regional companies' interest and investment as well as presented them with opportunities. Examples include the growth triangle negotiated by Singapore, Malaysia's state of Johor, and Indonesia's Riau Islands, which serves as a focus for economic growth and investment. Consequently, though Southeast Asian companies investing in the West's industrialized, information-rich economies gain the advantages of that abundant information when they do so, they have to deal with the informational void of their own region when conducting the great majority of their business operations in what they consider their primary markets.

This informational void, especially regarding the external environments of firms operating in the region, determines the strategic management style and procedures of the Overseas Chinese of Southeast Asia. The informational void also poses a serious challenge to traditional forms of strategic planning and management used by managers that operate in the industrialized countries' information-rich economies.

As we showed in the previous chapter, Western multinationals entering Southeast Asia cannot expect their Overseas Chinese competitors and potential strategic partners to behave as the Japanese do. The region also presents Western multinationals with substantial challenges to their traditional, information-rich, strategic-management techniques. In our next section, we will consider what information Western theorists generally consider desirable for strategic decisions. We will then present evidence of the Southeast Asian informational void and compare the available information with that available in the United States. We will finish with a discussion of the strategic-management and decision-making styles of Southeast Asian managers.

The informational void

Tables 4.1 and 4.2 present the results of a literature search of the ABI-Inform database – probably the most commonly available database of published articles worldwide. Four methodological issues in our study (Haley and Tan, 1996) need to be elaborated.

First, each topic title represents three to four topical key words. For example, 'Mkt Res' represents searches we conducted using the key words marketing research, market research, market data and marketing data. The key words represent many of the different kinds of information that strategic planners and executives use to understand their environments when they plan.

Second, we screened the results in Tables 4.1 and 4.2 to eliminate spurious hits unrelated to management issues and to ensure that the articles addressed the subject matter, or its application, in the countries we searched. The most common problem of this sort related to Vietnam where many articles profiling particular US executives or firms mentioned the executives as Vietnam War veterans or the firm's Vietnam War related activities; however, as strategic planners rarely consider such factors as important, we eliminated such hits from the two tables.

Third, we conducted the research only on the ten ASEAN (Association of Southeast Asian Nations) countries; yet, all available

Table 4.1   Academic business articles on Southeast Asia

Period	Brunei			Myanmar			Cambodia			Indonesia			Laos		
	A	B	C	A	B	C	A	B	C	A	B	C	A	B	C
Topic															
Marketing	0	0	0	0	0	0	0	1	0	1	8	2	0	1	0
Pricing	0	0	0	0	0	0	0	0	0	0	3	1	0	0	0
Promotion	0	0	0	0	0	0	0	0	0	0	0	0	0	0	0
Distrib	0	1	0	0	0	0	0	1	0	1	1	2	0	1	0
Prod Dev	0	0	0	0	0	0	0	0	0	0	0	1	0	0	0
Channels	0	0	0	0	0	0	0	0	0	0	0	0	0	0	0
Buyer Beh	0	0	0	0	0	0	0	0	0	0	0	0	0	0	0
Cons Beh	0	0	0	0	0	0	0	0	0	0	2	0	0	0	0
Demograph	0	0	0	0	0	0	0	0	0	1	1	0	0	0	0
Advert	0	0	0	0	0	0	0	0	0	0	2	0	0	0	0
Prod Mgt	0	0	0	0	0	0	0	0	0	0	0	0	0	0	0
Sales Mgt	0	0	0	0	0	0	0	0	0	0	0	0	0	0	0
In-store	0	0	0	0	0	0	0	0	0	0	0	0	0	0	0
Bus Res	0	0	0	0	0	0	0	0	0	0	0	0	0	0	0
Mgt Res	0	0	0	0	0	0	0	0	0	0	0	0	0	0	0
Mkt Res	0	0	0	0	0	0	0	0	0	0	0	1	0	0	0
Cons Res	0	0	0	0	0	0	0	0	0	0	0	0	0	0	0
Ind Mkt	0	0	0	0	0	0	0	0	0	0	2	0	0	0	0
Tran/Log	0	0	0	0	0	0	0	0	0	2	0	1	0	0	0
Strat Mgt	0	0	0	0	0	0	0	0	0	0	1	0	0	0	0
Mgt Decis	0	0	0	0	0	0	0	0	0	0	0	0	0	0	0
Culture	1	1	0	0	0	0	0	0	0	1	4	1	0	0	0
Media Hab	0	0	0	0	0	0	0	0	0	0	0	0	0	0	0
Mass Comm	0	0	0	0	0	0	0	0	0	0	0	0	0	0	0
Strat Plan	0	0	0	0	0	0	0	0	0	0	2	0	0	0	0
Total	1	2	0	0	0	0	0	2	0	6	26	9	0	2	0

Table 4.1   (continued)

Period	Malaysia			Philippines			Singapore			Thailand			Vietnam		
	A	B	C	A	B	C	A	B	C	A	B	C	A	B	C
Topic															
Marketing	3	5	9	0	1	0	9	13	11	3	11	5	0	1	0
Pricing	2	2	1	0	0	0	2	1	0	0	0	1	0	0	0
Promotion	0	0	0	0	0	0	2	2	3	0	0	0	0	0	0
Distrib	2	2	5	0	0	0	1	10	1	1	2	2	0	1	1
Prod Dev	0	0	0	0	0	0	1	0	1	0	1	0	0	0	0
Channels	0	0	0	0	0	0	0	0	0	0	1	0	0	0	0
Buyer Beh	0	0	0	0	0	0	0	0	0	0	0	0	0	0	0
Cons Beh	1	0	0	0	0	0	2	3	2	0	4	1	0	0	0
Demograph	7	2	3	0	0	0	4	2	2	2	2	1	0	0	0
Advert	1	3	2	0	0	0	2	2	5	0	2	1	0	0	0
Prod Mgt	0	0	0	0	0	0	0	0	0	0	0	0	0	0	0
Sales Mgt	0	0	0	0	0	0	0	0	0	0	0	0	0	0	0
In-store	0	0	0	0	0	0	0	0	0	0	0	0	0	0	0
Bus Res	0	0	0	0	0	0	0	0	0	0	1	1	0	0	0
Mgt Res	0	0	0	0	0	0	0	0	0	0	0	0	0	0	0
Mkt Res	0	0	2	0	0	0	5	1	4	0	0	1	0	0	0
Cons Res	0	0	0	0	0	0	1	1	0	0	1	0	0	0	0
Ind Mkt	0	0	0	0	0	0	0	0	0	0	0	0	0	0	1
Tran/Log	3	1	0	0	0	0	5	3	1	2	1	2	0	0	0
Strat Mgt	0	1	0	0	0	0	0	3	0	0	1	0	0	0	0
Mgt Decis	0	0	0	0	0	0	0	1	0	0	0	0	0	0	0
Culture	1	2	2	0	0	0	5	11	9	2	6	7	0	0	1
Media Hab	0	0	0	0	0	0	0	0	0	0	0	0	0	0	0
Mass Comm	0	0	0	0	0	0	0	0	1	0	0	0	0	1	0
Strat Plan	1	3	1	0	0	0	0	7	9	0	3	0	0	0	1
Total	21	21	25	0	1	0	39	60	49	9	36	20	0	3	4

Periods: A = 1987–89

B = 1990–93

C = 1994–mid-1995

Table 4.2 Business articles on Southeast Asia

Period	Brunei			Myanmar			Cambodia			Indonesia			Laos		
	A	B	C	A	B	C	A	B	C	A	B	C	A	B	C
Topic															
Marketing	0	0	0	0	1	0	0	1	0	3	39	36	0	2	0
Pricing	0	0	0	1	0	0	0	0	1	1	4	1	0	0	2
Promotion	0	0	0	0	0	0	0	0	0	0	2	0	0	0	0
Distrib	1	2	0	0	0	0	0	1	1	2	20	11	0	1	1
Prod Dev	0	0	0	0	0	0	0	0	0	0	5	3	0	0	0
Channels	0	0	0	0	0	0	0	0	0	0	0	0	0	0	0
Buyer Beh	0	0	0	0	0	0	0	0	0	0	0	0	0	0	0
Cons Beh	0	0	0	0	1	1	0	0	1	1	4	0	0	0	1
Demograph	0	0	0	0	0	0	0	0	0	2	6	0	0	0	0
Advert	0	0	1	0	1	2	0	0	1	0	15	5	0	2	1
Prod Mgt	0	0	0	0	0	0	0	0	0	0	0	0	0	0	0
Sales Mgt	0	0	0	0	0	0	0	0	0	0	0	0	0	0	0
In-store	0	0	0	0	0	0	0	0	0	0	0	0	0	0	0
Bus Res	0	0	0	0	0	0	0	0	0	1	0	0	0	0	0
Mgt Res	0	0	0	0	0	0	0	0	0	0	0	0	0	0	0
Mkt Res	0	0	0	0	0	0	0	0	0	0	1	1	0	0	0
Cons Res	0	0	0	0	0	0	0	0	0	0	0	0	0	0	0
Ind Mkt	0	0	0	0	0	0	0	0	0	0	3	0	0	0	0
Tran/Log	0	0	0	0	0	0	0	1	0	5	19	10	0	1	2
Strat Mgt	0	0	0	0	0	0	0	0	0	0	1	0	0	0	2
Mgt Decis	0	0	0	0	0	0	0	0	0	0	0	0	0	0	0
Culture	1	1	1	0	1	0	0	0	0	1	9	6	0	4	1
Media Hab	0	0	0	0	0	0	0	0	0	0	0	0	0	0	0
Mass Comm	0	0	0	0	1	0	0	0	0	0	0	0	0	1	0
Strat Plan	0	1	0	0	0	0	0	0	0	0	8	1	0	0	0
Total	2	4	2	1	5	3	0	3	4	16	136	74	0	11	10

Table 4.2 (continued)

Period	Malaysia			Philippines			Singapore			Thailand			Vietnam		
	A	B	C	A	B	C	A	B	C	A	B	C	A	B	C
Topic															
Marketing	16	61	32	0	1	0	20	21	16	6	23	12	0	10	17
Pricing	5	7	5	0	0	0	3	2	1	1	6	1	0	2	1
Promotion	0	1	8	0	0	0	4	5	3	2	1	0	0	0	1
Distrib	8	22	9	0	0	0	5	18	3	6	8	6	0	1	6
Prod Dev	2	5	0	0	0	0	1	3	5	0	2	0	0	1	0
Channels	0	0	0	0	0	0	0	0	0	1	2	0	0	1	0
Buyer Beh	0	0	0	0	0	0	0	0	0	0	0	0	0	0	0
Cons Beh	1	2	0	0	0	0	2	4	3	0	7	2	0	0	1
Demograph	7	4	3	0	0	0	5	6	2	2	6	2	0	1	1
Advert	5	11	6	0	0	0	5	10	16	2	12	5	0	7	10
Prod Mgt	0	1	0	0	0	0	0	0	0	0	0	0	0	0	0
Sales Mgt	0	0	0	0	0	0	0	0	0	0	0	0	0	0	0
In-store	0	0	0	0	0	0	0	0	0	0	0	0	0	1	0
Bus Res	0	0	0	0	0	0	0	0	0	0	1	1	0	0	0
Mgt Res	0	0	0	0	0	0	0	0	0	0	0	0	0	0	0
Mkt Res	0	0	2	0	0	0	5	2	4	0	1	1	0	0	0
Cons Res	0	0	0	0	0	0	1	1	0	0	1	0	0	0	0
Ind Mkt	0	0	0	0	0	0	0	0	0	0	0	0	0	2	2
Tran/Log	6	5	9	0	0	1	10	21	7	5	10	9	1	4	14
Strat Mgt	0	1	0	0	0	0	0	4	0	0	1	0	0	0	0
Mgt Decis	0	0	0	0	0	0	0	1	0	0	0	0	0	0	0
Culture	2	9	9	0	0	0	5	17	13	5	12	13	0	3	4
Media Hab	0	0	0	0	0	0	0	0	0	0	0	0	0	0	0
Mass Comm	0	1	0	0	0	0	0	0	1	0	1	1	0	2	0
Strat Plan	1	6	7	0	0	0	1	17	9	3	11	3	0	1	4
Total	53	136	90	0	1	1	67	126	83	33	105	56	1	36	61

Periods: A = 1987–89
B = 1990–93
C = 1994–mid-1995

evidence indicates that we can generalize our results to Taiwan despite its size, importance and level of development.

Finally, though our database has a Western, even an English-language bias, this bias remains consistent over the entire period of study. Alternatively, Southeast Asia's relative economic importance to the West has increased over the period covered by this study. Thus, regardless of the study's inherent regional and linguistic bias, if business authors and researchers reflect the topics' relative importance, coverage of Southeast Asian markets should increase relative to coverage of the US markets or to other economic markets worldwide.

Ironically, the results reveal that business researchers have concentrated on Singapore, the smallest state geographically in the region, with the second-smallest population and, with one of the smallest regional economies. Although Singapore has the wealthiest, most advanced economy and domestic market structure in the region, it also probably has the most homogenized and westernized business communities and environments outside of North America, Western Europe, Australia or New Zealand.

To compare the Southeast Asian, Taiwanese and US markets, consider the data in Table 4.3. In terms of population, GDP, and geographic size, we can see that the GDP of Southeast Asia, at US$2,099.6 billion, represents 27.6 per cent of the US economy's US$7,610 billion. Southeast Asia also has a significantly smaller landmass, representing only 47.5 per cent of the US landmass. But, the region has a significantly larger population, approximately 200 per cent that of the United States.

For adequate strategic planning in the United States, Western firms often gather and analyze specific data relating to market segments, various corporate and societal cultures, and myriad economic, competitive, political, and legal environments. These data assume far more complexity for Southeast Asia. The United States arguably constitutes the most culturally diverse single nation in the world; however, its legal, political, and economic environments vary little across states. Conversely, each country in Southeast Asia has its own rich historical, cultural, linguistic, economic, legal and ethnic backgrounds. Of the eleven nations, only Thailand escaped colonialism. Thus, Southeast Asian countries exhibit myriad differences in local cultures originating from their diverse histories and populations. Given the region's

Table 4.3 A comparison of Southeast Asia and Taiwan with the United States

	Population[1]	GDP[2] (billions)	Area (sq. mi.)
Brunei	299,939	4.6[3]	2,226
Myanmar	46,821,943	47.0[3]	261,228
Cambodia	11,163,861	7.0[3]	70,238
Indonesia	209,774,138	710.9[3]	741,052
Laos	5,116,959	5.2[3]	91,429
Malaysia	20,491,303	193.6[3]	127,584
Philippines	76,103,564	179.7[3]	115,860
Singapore	3,440,693	72.2[4]	247
Thailand	59,450,818	455.7[4]	198,115
Vietnam	75,123,880	108.7[4]	127,246
Taiwan	21,699,776	315.0[3]	13,892
Total	529,486,874	2,099.6	1,749,117
United States	267,954,764	7,610.0[4]	3,679,192
Comparison	197.6%	27.6%	47.5%

[1] US Census Bureau, World Population Estimates, 1997.
[2] In US dollars.
[3] 1995 figure.
[4] 1996 figure.

inherent complexity, the research and publication on the region seem exceedingly small.

Figure 4.1 shows that though little information exists on Southeast Asia, the information has increased sharply. To gauge changes over time, we compared the number of publications on Southeast Asia with those for the United States and for the total number of publications the database held for the search topics regardless of geographic limitations.

However, Table 4.4 indicates the imbalance in the relative amount of published knowledge about the United States and Southeast Asia. Looking from Table 4.4A through 4.4B and 4.4C, we notice the

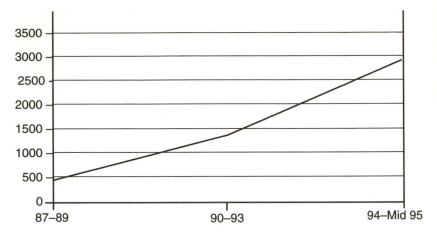

Figure 4.1 Average number of Southeast Asian publications per year

increase in publications on Southeast Asia from one time period to the next. However, total publications and publications on the United States also increase substantially.[1] The combined increases confound our ability to determine whether the increased numbers of publications on Southeast Asia represent an actual increase in the proportion of articles covering the region. Such a proportional increase would reflect the region's increasing economic and political importance. If the increase merely demonstrates an increase in the numbers of publications, without an actual increase in the proportion of total publications, the increase probably only reflects an increase in total articles published, and/or an increase in publications tracked by ABI-Inform. By taking the percentages of publications listed in Tables 4.4A, 4.4B, and 4.4A, and subtracting them from the percentages in Tables 4.4.B, 4.4C, and 4.4C, respectively, one gets a series of positive (+), negative (–), or no-change (/) results. A signs test can then be used to determine if actual increases in publications have occurred relative to the United States and to total publications. If publications on Southeast Asia have continued to increase significantly, relative to the

---

1. Please recall that the base of information in Table 4.4 is different than in Tables 4.1 and 4.2. The number of publications on the United States for some topic areas is so large that it was impossible to screen them as we did for Tables 4.1 and 4.2. To ensure comparability, the publications for Southeast Asia are also the unscreened totals.

Table 4.4A Southeast Asia business publications trends –
Period A: 1987–89

Topic	Southeast Asia			United States	
	Number	% of US	% of total	Number	Total on topic
Marketing	79	2.9	0.56	2,681	14,012
Pricing	16	2.6	0.48	612	3,367
Promotion	20	3.4	0.66	585	3,037
Distribution	37	2.6	0.55	1,416	6,710
Product development	5	0.9	0.22	505	2,306
Channel of distribution	4	3.1	0.64	130	626
Buyer behavior	0	0.0	0.00	1	13
Consumer behavior	3	1.5	0.23	196	1,280
Demographics	15	2.4	0.76	629	1,983
Advertising	22	1.6	0.36	1,390	6,070
Product management	0	0.0	0.00	29	226
Sales management	0	0.0	0.00	15	222
Point of purchase	1	1.8	0.27	56	370
Business research/data	2	3.7	0.64	54	311
Management research/data	0	0.0	0.00	16	288
Market research/data	11	13.1	0.35	84	3,183
Consumer research/data	1	4.3	0.44	23	228
Business to business	1	1.1	0.14	87	697
Transport/logistics	31	4.4	1.14	698	2,715
Strategic management	1	2.5	0.28	40	357
Management decision making	0	0.0	0.00	13	118
Culture	30	4.7	1.14	645	2,642
Media habits	0	0.0	0.00	4	13
Mass media/ communication	1	4.2	0.86	24	116
Strategic planning	15	2.4	0.43	632	3,528
Total	1,391	4.9		28,443	

Table 4.4B Southeast Asia business publications trends –
Period B: 1990–93

Topic	Southeast Asia			United States	
	Number	% of US	% of total	Number	Total on topic
Marketing	219	1.0	0.75	21,174	29,297
Pricing	41	0.9	0.63	4,661	6,530
Promotion	76	1.9	1.35	4,100	5,648
Distribution	117	1.3	0.88	8,739	13,271
Product development	32	0.6	0.47	5,321	6,852
Channel of distribution	10	1.4	1.00	725	999
Buyer behavior	0	0.0	0.00	21	31
Consumer behavior	17	1.2	0.71	1,474	2,387
Demographics	25	0.9	0.73	2,789	3,422
Advertising	73	0.6	0.46	13,164	15,984
Product management	1	0.5	0.34	186	298
Sales management	0	0.0	0.00	195	260
Point of purchase	2	0.3	0.25	685	812
Business research/data	1	0.2	0.13	442	787
Management research/data	0	0.0	0.00	212	491
Market research/data	19	0.7	0.39	2,789	4,828
Consumer research/data	19	10.4	5.54	183	343
Business to business	8	1.1	0.78	721	1,021
Transport/logistics	83	1.8	1.12	4,726	7,406
Strategic management	5	1.0	0.61	482	826
Management decision making	1	1.2	0.65	83	154
Culture	111	3.0	1.81	3,707	6,142
Media habits	0	0.0	0.00	20	30
Mass media/ communication	2	0.9	0.68	226	296
Strategic planning	162	2.4	1.57	6,784	10,320
Total	5,444	2.5		216,016	

Table 4.4C Southeast Asia business publications trends –
Period C: 1994–mid-1995

Topic	Southeast Asia			United States	
	Number	*% of US*	*% of total*	*Number*	*Total on topic*
Marketing	155	1.0	0.65	15,739	23,766
Pricing	29	1.0	0.77	2,894	3,750
Promotion	60	2.3	1.63	2647	3,672
Distribution	63	1.0	.73	6472	8,683
Product development	17	0.3	0.34	4,974	4,974
Channel of distribution	4	0.5	0.42	845	958
Buyer behavior	0	0.0	0.00	11	14
Consumer behavior	9	1.0	0.70	867	1,292
Demographics	10	0.6	0.55	1,573	1,826
Advertising	60	0.5	0.36	11,461	16,490
Product management	0	0.0	0.00	109	153
Sales management MGT	0	0.0	.00	254	280
Point of purchase	2	0.4	.37	457	545
Business research/data	3	1.1	0.76	262	393
Management research/data	1	0.6	0.29	179	350
Market research/data	11	0.7	0.44	1,512	2,483
Consumer research/data	0	0.0	0.00	108	156
Business to business	7	1.4	1.13	483	620
Transport/logistics	64	1.9	1.29	3,361	4,978
Strategic management	1	0.3	0.21	324	477
Management decision making	0	0.0	0.00	32	53
Culture	91	3.6	2.39	2,521	3,808
Media habits	0	0.0	0.00	8	11
Mass media/ communication	2	1.5	0.89	134	225
Strategic planning	83	1.3	1.02	6,197	8,126
Total	4,430	2.3		189,610	

Table 4.4D The signs test

Topic	Compared to US			Compared to total		
	B–A	C–B	C–A	B–A	C–B	C–A
Marketing	–	/	–	+	–	+
Pricing	–	+	–	+	+	+
Promotion	–	+	–	+	+	+
Distribution	–	–	–	+	–	+
Product development	–	–	–	+	–	+
Channel distribution	–	–	–	+	–	–
Buyer behavior	/	/	/	/	/	/
Consumer behavior	–	–	–	+	–	+
Demographics	–	–	–	–	–	–
Advertising	–	–	–	+	–	/
Production management	+	–	/	+	–	/
Sales management	/	/	/	/	/	/
Point of purchase	–	+	–	–	+	+
Business research/data	–	+	+	–	+	+
Management research/data	/	+	–	/	+	+
Market research/data	–	/	–	+	+	+
Consumer research/data	+	–	+	–	–	–
Business to business	/	+	–	+	+	+
Transport/logistics	–	+	–	–	+	+
Strategic management	–	–	/	+	–	–
Management decision making	+	–	–	+	–	/
Culture	–	+	/	+	+	+
Media habits	/	/	–	/	/	/
Mass media/communication	–	+	–	–	/	+
Strategic planning	/	–	–	+	–	+
Total on region	–	–	–			

Number of pluses	3	9	2	15	9	15
Z scores for + signs	–3.92	–1.57	–4.31	–1.41	–1.98	1.41
Probability	0.00	0.058	0.000	0.079	0.024	0.079
Number of minuses	17	12	19	6	12	4
Z scores for – signs	1.57	–0.39	2.35	–3.68	–0.28	–5.72
Probability	0.058	0.348	0.009	0.000	0.390	0.00

United States or to total publications, positive (+) signs should dominate; if not, negative (–) signs or no-change (/) signs should dominate. Perfect chance would be represented by equal numbers of positive and negative signs. A Z-score can then be developed to determine if the variance from chance is significant.

In considering Table 4.4D, we see that plus signs do not dominate; most signs emerge negative when comparing publications on Southeast Asia with publications on the United States. In testing the Z-score for plus signs, we found that the negative trend runs extensively and deeply. Even after the widespread drop in publications from period A to period B, the drop between period B and period C remains significant at the 0.06 level. Though the second score does not provide the strongest endorsement, considering the drop in the number of plus signs between the first two periods, it remains significant. As plus and minus are not mutually exclusive, and as a substantial number of no changes occur in our middle column, we conducted a second signs test for minus signs. Here we found that changes between periods A and B are significant only at the 0.06 level, and that changes between periods B and C are not significant at all. Changes between the beginning and end of the time period studied showed that the negative trend in coverage is highly significant.

When comparing publications on Southeast Asia with total publications on the topics, the region fares better. Overall, a trend of increased coverage on Southeast Asia has occurred relative to total publications. Interestingly, both the overall increase, as measured by the number of pluses, and the increase between period A and period B, as measured by the number of pluses, are significant only at the 0.08 level, and virtually all of the overall increase comes in the first period (B – A). In comparing the change in publications between periods B and C, we find that the number of pluses is significantly (at the 0.02 level) below chance. Though none of the analyses show the number of minuses above the chance level (12.5 in this instance), they would seem to indicate that the 1990s have seen a leveling off, or perhaps even some reduction, in the relative number of articles published on Southeast Asia. This trend occurred regardless of the much greater interest the private sector has shown in the area through its investments in the region. With increasing foreign investment in the region aimed at serving local markets, rather than markets in the industrialized countries, the overall trend in research and publication is puzzling.

Operating in an informational void

The analyses indicate that Southeast Asia as a region does indeed constitute an informational void. The tables also show that in the region, the more industrially developed nations, such as Singapore, received better coverage than the less industrially developed ones regardless of their markets' relative sizes. Generally, information on any country does not correspond with its stage of economic development. When one compares Singapore with New Zealand, another island nation, which though significantly larger geographically, has about the same population, one notices much more research and data published on New Zealand than on Singapore. Yet Singapore ranks higher than the UK, Australia and New Zealand in per capita income worldwide. Consequently, levels of relative economic development do not explain adequately the informational void in Southeast Asia.

Though we have thoroughly developed discussions on the history and cultural influences of the Overseas Chinese, we can better understand the development and maintenance of the informational void by examining an additional aspect of the history of business development in the region – the interactions between the major types of regional businesses. Southeast Asia has historically had three major clusters of large businesses: state-owned or government-linked corporations (GLCs); the Overseas Chinese family businesses; and multinational corporations. In more recent years a fourth group has arisen, the Overseas Indian family businesses. All four groups have prospered through operating in the informational void for various reasons. The groups, rather than insisting that the environment conform to traditional strategic management perceptions of desirable data, chose to adjust their strategies and management accordingly, and coped quite adequately with their environments. They had different reasons and different needs, but achieved similar end results.

We will first consider the GLCs. These organizations have played major roles in the development of many industries in their respective home countries, and have in some instances, contributed a great deal to their respective nations' economic development. Few are actually government owned, but usually started as suppliers of products or services in protected, if not monopolistic, domestic market environments. With strong domestic demand caused by the tremendous economic growth in the region, and lack of serious competition, many of these businesses flourished; many others evolved into inefficient dinosaurs kept alive in apparently good health by the region's economies more than anything else. For such businesses, their countries' plans for economic growth and development dictated their strategic planning and management patterns. Hence, market information and industry data never constituted critical success factors.

We will next consider the foreign multinationals, which generally arrived to the region much later. European trading houses have existed for decades in Southeast Asia. Indeed, many of the old European international trading houses have older pedigrees in Asia than the Overseas Chinese companies. However, the trading houses did not shape Southeast Asian business environments as much as the manufacturing-based multinationals that entered the region in large numbers much more recently. The manufacturing-based multinationals from the industrialized regions have served as key contributors to the export-led economic growth of many of the region's countries. Since the end of World War II, when multinationals started to rationalize their manufacturing policies worldwide based on cost, Southeast Asia has been a favorite location for their investments. Southeast Asia provided everything the multinationals wanted: attractive tax incentives on top of low tax rates; investment benefits; and cheap, but trainable and increasingly educated labor offered by host countries. Consequently, multinationals poured increasing amounts of investment into the region in each of the decades that followed World War II and transferred some of their manufacturing operations there.

Multinationals' managers generally had little difficulty making decisions on relocating to Southeast Asia. In many instances, host governments compiled and offered to the multinationals the information relevant to make such decisions. As the multinationals did not design their manufacturing operations to serve local markets, they did not need local market information. To obtain production-cost advantages in their worldwide operations the multinationals primarily needed accounting and cost data; they also required acceptable port facilities to ship the manufactured goods intended primarily for export markets. Such internal decisions to maximize operational efficiency require much less data on local environments than decisions to serve local markets. Hence, the multinationals' managers did not encounter the unavailability of information on Southeast Asian markets; or, they did not consider the informational void important as rationalizing production costs surmounted in importance to sales to local markets.

We will now consider the Overseas Chinese family businesses. The Overseas Chinese family businesses constitute probably the single, most-dominant, private, business grouping in Southeast Asia. As we saw in Chapter One, the Overseas Chinese generally represent a relatively small minority among most Southeast Asian local populations; yet their economic influence in the local economies far exceeds their physical numbers. Today, they are wielding their various networks to extend their reach beyond their traditional stomping grounds in Southeast Asia to many parts of the world. For example, Acer computers holds the second-largest market share in Mexico and assumes a competitive position in its industry in many other economically advanced developing nations. Formosa Plastics, Tiger Beer, Creative Technology, and New York's famed Plaza Hotel constitute just some of the famous brand names that the Overseas Chinese businessmen own.

Historically, many Overseas Chinese, such as Singapore's Goh Cheng Liang, founder of the Wuthelam Group, started their businesses as merchants and traders. As a general rule, once the Overseas Chinese established some degree of financial stability, they

---

Stan Shih – drawing aces with Acer

Stan Shih, founder and chairman of Acer Computers of Taiwan built the company from a US$25,000, 11-employee start-up to the US$7 billion company of today. Acer is the world's fourth-largest maker of personal computers and PC parts, and one of Taiwan's few globally recognized brand names.

Shih had a humble start. He still recalls the day that his incense-maker father died and he had to help his widowed mother sell duck eggs, watermelon seeds and lottery tickets. Acer started out in 1976 as Multitech; its main business then involved trading and consulting services for Taiwan's young information technology industry. He got into the computer industry by

---

supplying 'made in Taiwan' computers to major PC makers around the world – but decided that to attain viability in the future PC industry, a company had to market its own brand name PCs. The road to create and to establish one's brand name in an industry dominated by names such as IBM, Compaq, NEC and Hewlett-Packard, especially for a small player in the industry such as Acer from a market not known for high technology, such as Taiwan, appeared bumpy to say the least. Shih started by achieving the number 1 or 2 market position in several rapidly developing markets such as Indonesia, Malaysia, Mexico, South Africa and a host of other emerging markets. The ultimate challenge of making it to the top league of PC companies in the US market came true with the launch of the Aspire line of PCs in 1995. Acer introduced Aspire as a radically new-looking PC with soft shapes, cool curves and dark, rich colors such as charcoal gray and emerald green; Aspire vaulted Acer from number 9 in the US market into the top five best-selling lines.

Since 1995, Acer has been making waves in various aspects of manufacturing and management practices. It is now highly regarded as an innovative competitor to be taken seriously in information technology. Shih looks at Acer as 'The Dragon Dream'. He said, 'This dream is not mine, but is derived from a sense of the general direction and aspirations of colleagues and young people' (*Asian Business*, September, 1993, p. 51). He and his team built a business empire known as the fast-food model of PC manufacturing. Shih borrowed a concept from the fast-food industry: the company ships pre-processed ingredients to outlets to minimize preparation time; and the company makes the product just-in-time to maintain freshness and consistency. Acer manufactures components, such as caseworks, power supplies, keyboards and monitors at its plants in Taiwan and Malaysia and ships them to regional assembly facilities. Acer air freights more technology and price-sensitive items such as motherboards, while locally procuring other components such as disk drives and memory chips.

Today, Acer forms a network of independent companies (each with substantial local shareholdings in the respective company's country) linked together to pursue Acer's 'Dragon Dream'.

would quickly move into property-related businesses, and before long, diversified into almost any business deemed profitable. As discussed in the previous chapter, Robert Kuok of Malaysia presents an extremely successful example of this unique diversification; his investments cover every continent save Africa and Antarctica and his businesses range from commodities trading to beverages, utilities and infrastructural projects to hotels and resorts, media and cinema to plantations. The Overseas Chinese businesses generally display an intuitive, entrepreneurial, and fast decision-making style, and paternalistic management. To understand how fast the Overseas Chinese act when they scent a good investment, consider Wuthelam Group's move into New Zealand property development. One of the Group's most senior executives with long-time experience in the firm's property development business, while visiting New Zealand saw a property in receivership. When interviewed for this book, he described his actions in the following manner:

> An investment of 17 million Kiwi dollars may seem like a lot, but the original developers had already invested 10 million in infrastructure, had already developed one marina on the property successfully. The receiver's valuation on the land was 25 million dollars, but I had been able to bargain them down. In effect then, we would only be paying 7 million for the land itself as it had 10 million in improvements. With 7 million, I take a chance. Paying 8 million below the valuation, I also had some leeway. Based on my experience it would have been difficult to lose money on the property. Now, with greater experience and knowledge about the New Zealand market and the overall situation, we are expanding and the final investment will be over 1 billion Kiwi dollars.

Due to their low levels of formal education, especially of business education, the founders and trusted senior executives of many Overseas Chinese businesses made decisions to invest, to grow, and to compete almost solely on the basis of business sense, experience, and their individual propensities to take risks. The requirements of traditional Western business information and detailed analyses of business ventures rarely occurred, if at all. The above example on Wuthelam exemplifies every aspect of the traditional decision-making process. New Asian Emperor, Robert Kuok, on whom *Forbes* magazine bestowed the title, 'The World's Shrewdest Businessman', elaborated on his prejudice against hiring MBAs and using their decision-making

Goh Cheng Liang –
Wuthelam Group: A family company professionalizing

Goh Cheng Liang was born to a poor family. In a rare interview given to the *Business Times* of Singapore (26 September 1997), he recalled, 'my father was jobless. My mother was washing laundry, my sister was selling *soon kway* (a Chinese rice-noodle cake)'. His first business venture, the production of aerated water, ended in failure. His first major break came in 1949 when the British army was auctioning off surplus stocks of war material. He bought several barrels of 'rotten paint'. He then started mixing the paint with various colors and selling it under his own brand name, Pigeon Brand Paint. As the Korean War grew in intensity, his business blossomed.

When a joint venture to distribute paint broke up between Nippon Paint of Osaka, Sim Lim Group of Singapore, and Charoen Pokhphand (CP) Group of Thailand, Goh decided to continue on his own with Nippon Paint. He purchased a 60 per cent interest in the resulting joint venture. Nippon Paints' expansion in Asia, and its subsequent strong hold on the Asian markets is largely due to Goh's entrepreneurial drive.

He used his resulting fortune from the paint-distribution business to diversify into other businesses such as property and retailing. Goh also started the Mount Elizabeth Hospital, a premier private healthcare center for the region which he sold off some years ago.

Although Goh has made Nippon Paint a household name in Asia, he often attributes his success to luck. Sources close to him attribute his success to his management style and his ability to judge how best to use people to obtain the best returns from their abilities. A strong believer in his philosophy, 'Have faith in your staff, they will bring in results', he has created many millionaires among his loyal staff.

Today, the Wuthelam Group no longer forms the typical paternalistically managed Chinese family company. A new influx of professional management, widely covered in the media, along with the return of his son, Goh Hup Jin, has created a new Wuthelam. With the recruitment of Koh Boon Hwee, the former managing director of Hewlett-Packard, Singapore,

Wuthelam is professionalizing at a rapid rate. Several Wuthelam Group companies have gone public, and Wuthelam is moving into the information technology industry as well.

Goh's genuine concern for his people is exemplified by his founding of a new company, Yenom, to house staff affected by the professionalization wave at Wuthelam. He said, 'Most of the old staff cannot work with the new, very logical management, that is why I had to start this new company to house all the people who are used to the same system as me' (*Business Times*, 26 September 1997). Interestingly, Yenom, the new company founded for the old staffers is doing well – demonstrating that the old style can work well even in this modern age.

techniques: 'When I hear somebody's got an MBA, I have a feeling of dread, because normally they come to me with an overpompous sense of their own importance. And no way are you going to prick that bubble, with the result that one day there will be a cave-in in their department. So, they learn painful lessons at my expense!' (*Forbes*, 28 July 1997, p. 94). On occasions when truly difficult decisions had to be made, and additional information was considered necessary, the Chinese businessmen usually depended upon their network of friends and/or well-connected government officials to supply them with the relevant information. Trust and loyalty formed central concerns: they still do. The traditional, hard data desired by Western strategic and operational planners is not necessary. The desired information frequently involved subjective views or beliefs that the businessmen used to increase confidence levels in their decisions.

The second generation of more modern Overseas Chinese executives often express the same doubts in the efficacy of market research as their predecessors. Stan Shih, founder and chairman of Acer Computers, a US$5 billion company, for instance, explained to us in an interview for this book that he relies on 'Gut Feel', though not on the gut feel of one person, not even if that gut feel is his own. Stan Shih believes in and relies on the collective gut feel of his team at the top of Acer Computers. Research to him is 'something which confirms the known'. He argues that:

You don't really need market data and information. As each decision often is not big. Although (at the founding of Acer) there was risk, the smallness of the project and the decision made the decision-making relatively easy.

And as for the use of market research:

We use it in a small way. We believe in doing things quickly. We do discuss things amongst ourselves a lot, it is like a team kind of gut feel. We implement and change things quickly. It is all implementation in the market place.

This somewhat holistic, yet intuitive, decision-making style corresponds well to an information-scarce environment and to the competitive situation in which most founders of today's great Overseas Chinese empires found themselves. As one New Asian Emperor interviewed for this book, but who prefers to remain anonymous, said:

Making decisions without feasibility studies is not a Chinese trait, it is a decision-making trait which is common to any who enter business under conditions of scarcity. If you take the risk, maybe you lose your money, but maybe you don't. If you invest in the research or feasibility study, you don't have any chance to win, you no longer have the money to invest.

The network system also served to exclude effectively new entrants who lacked the Overseas Chinese business community's experience and contacts. For instance, many Southeast Asian banks have historically had community bases – that is, they serve particular groups, or networks, of people, not groups of people who live within specific geographic areas; these community bases continue today, creating barriers to entry in some instances. For example, as noted in Chapter 3, individuals who apply for business loans from banks in Indonesia often find that all the information included in their application has been transferred to the banks' related companies in the same business as the applicants'; and, that the related companies have not only moved into the business, but have even implemented the business plans submitted with the application (East Asia Analytical Unit (EAAU), 1995)!

Many observers have attributed the rapid growth of many overseas Chinese family businesses in the region to their amazing speed of decision-making (Chu and MacMurray, 1993); this speed and ability to dominate access to information make the ability to seize major business opportunities possible. The tremendous speed with which the Wuthelam Group moved into New Zealand property development is an indication of just how fast the Overseas Chinese can move. As noted in previous chapters, they are not foolhardy. As a second, senior Wuthelam executive pointed out, the initial investment of 17 million Kiwi dollars was only '2 to 3 per cent of annual cash flow'. While they would have hated to lose the money, the company's viability would not have been affected by losing every penny of the invest- ment, something unlikely to occur as the acquisition cost approximated only about two thirds of the property's valuation by the court's receivers.

The above decision-making traits add up to a different way of doing business in Southeast and East Asia than that practiced in the West (Haley, G. T., 1997a, b; Haley and Haley, 1997; 1998; Haley and Tan, 1996; 1998; Hofstede, 1994). These differences greatly influence the Overseas Chinese networks' management and decision-making styles and practices. Researchers have posited various explanations for the differences that emerge between Asian and Western strategic decision-making. For example, Haley and Tan (1996) and Haley and Haley (1997) suggested competitive advantage as a possible explanation. The Overseas Chinese networks' abilities to exclude inexperienced and poorly connected competitors support this explanation. Also, many Overseas Chinese companies have continued to employ many of the same holistic decision-making practices after becoming large multinationals, and long after hiring experienced, Western-trained managers away from multinational competitors – further indicating that their strategic decision-making style provides a competitive advantage. The decision-making style, and the environments in which they prosper, also weaken marketing and distribution, the primary competitive strengths for many of their multinational com- petitors. Western multinationals have difficulties making decisions without hard data; marketing research precedes virtually every single major competitive move. Yet, in Southeast Asia, little of the desired data exists, and Asians often do not undertake or participate well in research programs. Hence, by promoting information scarcity, the Overseas Chinese businessmen deny to larger, more- technologically advanced Western multinationals with stronger brand names, an important advantage that they expect and generally have.

New Asian Emperors

Hofstede (1994) argued that ethnic and cultural factors accounted for differences in decision-making styles; alternatively, Haley and Stumpf (1989) found differences in decision-making traceable to personality types. Later, Haley, U. C. V. (1997) detected evidence of significant personality-type differences between managerial cadres from different countries thereby supporting Hofstede's arguments. Fei's (1992) work which traces cultural differences, including perceptions and ethics, to civilizational differences between the West and the East, also tends to support Hofstede's rationales.

A potent understanding of the Overseas Chinese networks' decision-making styles probably incorporates facets from all the different explanations. However, Haley and Tan's (1996) categorization of Asia (elaborated in the previous section) as an informational void relative to the amount of information available in industrialized economies lies unquestioned. This informational void we have argued has led to a unique, strategic-management style for many Asian companies. Consequently, the major differences in Asian decision-making stem from the information that Asian decision-makers have available and desire which differs significantly from that used by Western managers and strategic theorists (Haley, G.T., 1997a; Haley and Tan, 1996; 1998).

To be effective in Southeast Asia, Western managers need to study holistic/intuitive decision-making, and to learn it fast. Although social psychologists and pop gurus have studied differences between Eastern and Western thought processes, learning capabilities, and decision-making styles, little formal knowledge exists of Southeast Asia's holistic/intuitive decision-making styles. In part, this stems from the lack of management research in the region. Drawing on our observations and study of Asian executives, including the New Asian Emperors, and in consulting and executive development seminars, we propose several salient characteristics common to such an experience-based holistic/intuitive approach to decision-making. They are:

1 Hands-on experience
2 Transfer of knowledge
3 Qualitative information
4 Holistic information processing
5 Action-driven decision-making.

Hands-on experience

To make quick decisions comfortably, without detailed analyses of hard data, managers need extensive knowledge and experience in their strategic environments. The managers must almost always approximate hands-on, line managers who have experienced the companies' work routines and processes, and know first-hand the products, markets, business environments and industries. If the managers originate from staff, without sufficient exposure to the detailed workings of the trade, they will have difficulty putting things in perspective quickly enough to make timely decisions. Consequently, and quite commonly, many senior Chinese businessmen running huge companies remain active in all aspects of their businesses. Their levels of involvement appear necessary for executives to comfortably make the right decisions without data support.

Kazuo Wada (1992) furnished an example where a Chinese businessman in Hong Kong responded within fifteen minutes to an offer by Li Kai Shang, chairman of the Hutchinson/Cheung Kong conglomerate, to enter into a joint venture. The businessman's confidence in Li's judgement, his ability to trust Li's word, and importantly, his in-depth knowledge of the business and markets under consideration allowed him to make such a rapid decision.

In our interviews with two Wuthelam Group senior executives, both recounted the story of their recent New Zealand property investment. The first, traditionally trained executive pushed forward with the investment. The second, Goh Hup Jin, chairman of Nipsea Holdings, son of the founder and a Western-trained executive, worked in several large US companies prior to joining Wuthelam Group; the Asian business press often portrays him as leading the modernization drive at Wuthelam. Goh Hup Jin's comments shed interesting light on the younger generation of management among the New Asian Emperors. First, his comments indicate a basic continuation of the traditional management style of the older generation of Overseas Chinese management, although admittedly with some modifications. And second, his comments testify to the high degree of emotional and psychic involvement that the management style entails. Goh Hup Jin said:

> Would I have gone to New Zealand and made the same decision? No. But not because I would never decide that way, it is because I do not like the

property industry. Some industries are labors of love. To make a decision in that fashion, it must be in an industry which is a labor of love. If I had gone to New Zealand and encountered a similar situation in an industry I love, yes. I would make a decision in very much the same way.

Few metaphors better convey the necessity of a hands-on, intimate knowledge of an industry than to describe work in the industry as a 'labor of love'.

Transfer of knowledge

Managers often have difficulties making good decisions within new environmental contexts. However, in Southeast Asia, companies often successfully diversify into new businesses, totally different and considered non-core. This runs contrary to conventional business wisdom of staying within one's core business and pursuing related diversification.

For an executive to function and to succeed in a completely new industry, in which he or she has no prior experience, the executive must have the ability to make generalizations from past experiences. The executive must also be able to transfer those generalizations into the new contexts. The dexterity to extract knowledge and the perspective to help one to tackle new problems in different situations involve conceptualization skills different from analytical skills. Successful Southeast Asian executives have the ability to see the big picture, and to sense intuitively winners from losers. For example, in the 1960s, New Asian Emperor Li Kai Shang diversified from becoming Hong Kong's biggest plastic flower producer to one of Hong Kong's most successful property developers. One former employee recalled, 'Li's great ability was to look at a building or even a site and calculate how much it was worth'. Jake van der Kamp, investment strategist with HG Asia in Hong Kong added, 'He got better and better at the game' (*Asia Inc.*, January 1997, p. 46). Whether one believes or not in the continuation of this characteristic decision-making style, it is an accepted part of business activity in the region (Chu and MacMurray, 1993). Chu and MacMurray (1993) believe that this aspect of business in Southeast Asia must change; yet, many businessmen in the region feel it contributes importantly to their firms' growth. For example, Thailand's Charoen Pokhphand (CP

Group), owned by the Chearavanont family started in poultry farming, and has since branched out into property investments and telecommunications in order to continue its rapid growth rates. It has done so while maintaining levels of profitability almost unheard of in the West.

A senior Overseas Chinese businessman, one of the New Asian Emperors, explained the advantages of conglomerate diversification to us in the following fashion:

> You put an egg in a basket; you hope it grows; it may not, it may die; then you are poor again. You go back to work, save your money and start again. I put one egg in the basket; it grew and I had some money so I put another. I found that the more different eggs I put in the basket, the more opportunities I had to put more eggs in. Diversification brings opportunity, and opportunity brings growth.

Qualitative information

Southeast Asian executives appear to take unnecessary risks by not undertaking sufficient research or analysis before acting; however this appearance may prove misleading. The executives often process myriad bits of information and consider several alternatives in depth before they take action. They differ from their Western counterparts in that for the Southeast Asian executives the process may occur, almost completely, internally. Although their decision-making may contain high degrees of articulation, the Southeast Asian executives may not present the results in detailed, written, analytical forms.

When we asked Wee Ee Cheong, deputy president of the United Overseas Bank Group, how he goes about making his decisions, he responded that he:

> ...doesn't let figures influence his decisions. (He) looks at the business first, sizes up the staff (his bank's staff) who wrote the business report, how thorough they were in their research, what assumptions they made in arriving at their conclusion.
>
> (He) often looks at the business, the management; who is in charge (he likes to talk to people at all levels in the organization; often middle level people give him the best information for his decision); the qualitative aspects of the decision. Numbers often come last. They are used to confirm the decision rather than to arrive at the decision.

Interestingly, Wee Ee Cheong constitutes one of the second generation of Overseas Chinese managers, not a member of the founding generation. His father, chairman and CEO of the United Overseas Bank Group, Wee Cho Yaw, with whom we also discussed strategic-management approaches, takes an even-more qualitative approach in his decision-making.

Overseas Chinese executives almost always use external sources of information when making strategic decisions. Our experience indicates that executives will actively seek out information and search for the critical pieces that will impact their final decisions. However, executives are less likely to refer to documented evidence or data in published form. They prefer to use sources of often qualitative, even subjective information, such as friends, business associates, government officials, and other people in whose judgement they trust, and in whom they personally trust. They may often travel to local scenes to check personally on the reliability of local information, rather than rely on secondary information. Their contacts and connections among local sources often consist of people who can supply up-to-date, accurate information that may not be published. Such first-hand information from original sources may prove superior to any other available alternatives. Consequently, with hindsight, many of the decisions that the Southeast Asian executives make appear correct.

Network building goes beyond linking oneself to some senior government official or great industrialist. Southeast Asian businessmen, while criticized for not building their companies' internal bases of managerial talent, often seek out promising individuals who they feel will prove valuable contacts in the future. For example, several years ago, Liem Sioe Liong of the Salim Group, the largest, and one of the most successful of the Overseas Chinese conglomerates, met a young army lieutenant whom he thought showed promise. He maintained contact with the lieutenant, and offered him his support during his military, and subsequent political, career. The promising young lieutenant is now ex-President Suharto of Indonesia and remains Liem Sioe Liong's close friend and supporter.

Holistic information processing

Conventional analytical problem solving, as taught in business schools and universities, tends to stress sequential, systematic, and step-by-step approaches to solving problems and making decisions. This approach proves most effective when, at each step, managers can obtain the proper inputs for use. The approach may prove optimal in situations where managers can readily generate or purchase needed data. In an informational void situation, managers may find the approach unworkable.

Wee Cho Yaw, chairman of United Overseas Bank, indicated to us that some generational differences may exist among the New Asian Emperors' strategic decision-making styles. Before, limited data existed, but the information was in different forms. However, he said of the managers of his generation:

> We talk breakfast, lunch, and attend social functions to exchange views and ideas; market information is often exchanged in social settings. Business decisions are made after factoring in all these views and input. However, to a large extent decisions are made on gut feel and business acumen.

The experience-based intuitive model described above views the problem in totality; managers take general approaches to problems, define parameters intuitively, and explore solutions in holistic manners. Such intuitive models appear to resemble Asian thinking and learning processes. They form alternative modes of decision-making that work well in many situations, especially in those environments in which they have evolved.

Action-driven decision-making

Speed constitutes one key characteristic of decision-making in the Southeast Asian business context. Executives often make key decisions without consulting anyone. Their preferences appear to revolve around action. Several stories exist of well-known Southeast

Asian executives who decided on important matters in minutes and implemented the results almost immediately. The quickness also reflects the empowerment and accountability of the executives' actions. Executives often have great latitude in deciding matters. Long debates and committee meetings rarely occur.

The Overseas Chinese decision-making model does reflect an authoritative management style. However, when one person has responsibility in a situation, and the authority to make final judgement, a little authoritativeness can move things more quickly, get work done faster and allow adroit exploitation of opportunities. Tan Kah Kee, one of the giants of the Overseas Chinese community in this century, took an initial early gamble; he made the decision to buy 500 acres of uncleared jungle to plant with pineapples to supply his pineapple-canning factory. However, when he cleared the land, he decided to bet on future opportunities rather than on his past successes. Rather than planting pineapples, he planted rubber trees. He had to move fast to take advantage of all the new opportunities for rubber: the year was 1905 and as Tan Kah Kee saw automobiles assuming importance, he had no time to waste (Yong, 1986).

A final note

The informational void in Southeast Asia appears tangible. It exists because of the manner in which business has historically been conducted and because of participants' goals. As the key decision-makers have not actively sought out more objective, empirical data and information in the past, the region has remained an informational void. The network management system of the Overseas Chinese enjoys several unique characteristics; yet, as the Wuthelam Group's senior executives indicated to us, strategic factors of import in other parts of the world, such as resource scarcity, also influence the Overseas Chinese strategic decisions. Given these observations from the New Asian Emperors, one can more fully comprehend their strengths and weaknesses through a strategic-planning model which classifies their strategic processes. In our next chapter, we will present a conceptualization of strategic planning developed in the West which helps us better understand the New Asian Emperor's strategic decisions and managing for competitive advantage in Asia generally.

Chapter Five

Concepts of Strategic Management

'What belonged to our family 100 years ago still belongs to us. It is our culture not to risk what great-grandfather built.'

Vuttichai Wanglee referring to his great grandfather, Tan Siew-Wang, first of the great founding fathers to defeat the third generation curse of Chinese fortunes, quoted in the *International Herald Tribune*, 17 April 1998

Introduction

Researchers and the media have recently granted a great deal of coverage to Overseas Chinese companies and their management; yet, they have made very little effort to understand the strategic implications of the management style that the Overseas Chinese companies practice. Most have either tried to describe the decision-making processes, explain the styles' various consequences, or explain their origins and significance; but, neither researchers nor the media have placed the Overseas Chinese network's strategic decision-making style within any of strategic planning's theoretical constructs. Many argue that the Overseas Chinese do not conduct strategic planning. This is patently absurd, and any survey of Chinese businessmen will prove otherwise. In this chapter we will place the Overseas Chinese strategic-management style within established, strategic planning constructs known and practiced in the West for many years. By doing so, we enhance strategic understanding of the Overseas Chinese networks' capabilities, strengths and weaknesses. By reinterpreting their behaviors through familiar lenses, we heighten the predictability of the Overseas Chinese; those who study behavioral implications will have the tools to judge the 'uprightness' of the Overseas Chinese managers they encounter. We note here that the Confucian influences on management that we have identified influence virtually all Southeast and East Asian cultures, but in varying degrees: although the Overseas Chinese dominate business operations in the region, not all Southeast Asian managers are Overseas Chinese.

First, we briefly review some of the major, theoretical, strategic planning constructs. We then incorporate the Overseas Chinese managers' decision processes within these constructs. Finally, we propose a best-fit scenario of the Overseas Chinese strategic planning style; this scenario will enable companies and executives that compete against, or co-operate with the Overseas Chinese to understand and to judge, not only the managers' behaviors, but also the reception their own behaviors and background will have on them. This chapter will complete the strategic analysis section of our book, and prepare us to move forward into the final section on strategic implications.

Strategic planning and the networks

Unlike the Asian strategic environment and management style we elaborated in the previous chapter, a determining factor in Western management involves the virtually unlimited wealth of information available to anyone with the desire and wit to find and to use it. Table 5.1 (Haley, G. T., 1997) summarizes two of the dominant characteristics of strategic planning processes propounded by prominent theorists that assume importance in our discussion of the strategic planning of the Overseas Chinese. Most established understandings of strategic planning incorporate: (i) abundance and easy availability of data on companies' industries, markets, and

Table 5.1 Characteristics of the strategic planning processes

Strategic theorists	Staff/Line dependent	Data/Experience dependent
Hofer and Schendel	Staff	Data
Porter	Staff	Data
Prahalad and Hamel	Staff/Line	Data/Experience
Mintzberg	Staff/Line	Data/Experience

environments; and (ii) significant investments in staff to collect, to collate, and to analyze the data. The staff would then interpret the information generated and develop strategic recommendations for senior management.

Planning, classically

Charles Hofer and Dan Schendel (1978) are among the earliest conceptualizers of a classic, strategic planning process. Michael Porter also uses many of the same building blocks for planning and hence, they share many characteristics. First, their processes depend on abilities to acquire large amounts of relatively high-quality internal and external information. Also, their processes need a wealth of data because the planning demands analytical rationalism. To employ a system of analytical rationalism requires largely sequential collection, analysis and interpretation of data to generate the above-mentioned information. More high-quality data that can be fed into analytical schemes should, in these theories, generate increasingly higher quality analysis thereby aiding the managers to achieve higher quality decisions.

Managers collect, analyze and interpret the data within fixed, perceptual constructs of the relationships between the companies and their environments. These perceptual constructs collectively form underlying theories of how the world works, and should work, with respect to the managers' particular problems. By emphasizing threats and opportunities in the companies' external environments and the companies' own strengths and weaknesses, the classical planning processes assume that managers can measure and understand the relationships between their companies and the environments through collecting and analyzing data within the positivist framework. Several problems may confound these classical planning processes.

First, if the managers' perceptual constructs (their underlying theories of all the variables involved, their influences and interactions) have validity, then the companies' strategic plans may achieve success, but no guarantees exist. For effective planning, the data that the managers use should also reliably represent the strategies being planned. If significant errors surround understandings of important variables or their measurement, managers are unlikely to develop effective strategies.

Second, the processes depend largely on companies' possessing substantial staff to collect, to collate, and to analyze large amounts of data to understand business environments and decision situations, and then to generate recommendations for strategic action. Frequently, members of the companies' staff have little or no line-management or operational experience. Often, the staff's understanding of business situations revolve around their familiarity with analytical techniques and their collection and interpretation of data; the staff have little knowledge of the nuances of the business' operations, the business' relationships with stakeholders, or any direct familiarity and understanding of the business' markets. These strategic planning processes, that so many Western managers learn in the world's premier MBA programs, separate the companies' minds and hands (Mintzberg, 1987, 1994); usually, they have no place for the 'hearts' or 'guts' with which many of the New Asian Emperors (elaborated in the previous chapter) sense their strategic opportunities.

Henry Mintzberg (1987, 1994), in discussing the different styles of strategic planning, distinguished between two kinds of strategic activities – the hands' activities in planning and the mind's activities in planning. The classic strategic planning processes and concepts represent the mind's activities in planning because of their heavy dependence on staff and data. They require substantial investments in data acquisition, intense mining of that data for information, and the development of plans based upon interpretation of the information generated. However, planning of the mind does not require line-management experience; familiarity with problems associated with managing production lines or sales forces; direct knowledge and experience in dealing with the companies' markets; or direct interaction with the companies' customers or suppliers to understand their problems and manners of thinking. In fact, planning of the mind requires no direct responsibility for generating corporate profits. The staff analysts may have purely academic understandings of their businesses, markets and environments; their expertise lies in the analytical tools they employ, not in their experiential understandings of the businesses.

Developing core competencies

C. K. Prahalad and Gary Hamel probably constitute the most influential strategic planning theorists of the 1990s. Prahalad and Hamel, in their seminal 1990 article, argued for a more internal focus to companies' strategic planning. They contended that business' most successful planning efforts occur when companies' strategies exploit core competencies or key skills, refined and honed over the years in various business' activities. Prahalad and Hamel indicated that by design or by coincidence, successful companies develop collections of skills at which they excel, and which constitute the bases for their success. These key skills they termed the companies' core competencies.

In any industry or market, more than one set of skills can contribute to core competency; hence, different companies in the same industry and serving the same markets can possess different core competencies. The relative competitive advantages of different core competencies change over time because of various factors such as industrial, technological or product life cycles or basic and applied innovations in the industries. For skills to contribute to companies' core competencies, they must:

1 Provide potential access to various markets.
2 Make important contributions to the perceived benefits companies provide their customers.
3 Be difficult to imitate.

Unlike Hofer and Schendel, and Porter, Prahalad and Hamel make no pronouncements about how to plan. Strategic planning drawing on

core competencies may or may not depend on substantial investments in obtaining large amounts of high-quality information and on
huge staff. The Overseas Chinese companies obviously appear to
wield their skills to enhance their core competencies; Mintzberg's
concept of crafting strategy sheds more light on these strategic
behaviors.

Crafting strategies

Mintzberg (1987; 1994) and Mintzberg and Waters (1985) have
championed a different approach to strategic planning that draws on
the crafting of strategies.

Using the metaphor of a craftsman making pottery, Mintzberg
(1987) described strategic planning as involving both the minds and
hands. The minds' activities in strategic planning stress classical,
strategic planning activities such as SWOT analysis and value chain
analysis. He (1987) also argued that strategic planning remains
incomplete when it excludes either the minds' activities or the hands'
activities. He (1987) postulated that strategic planning consists of
minds and hands performing four activities:

1 Detecting discontinuities
2 Knowing the business
3 Managing patterns
4 Reconciling change and continuity.

Detecting discontinuities

Mintzberg argued that companies earn profits primarily during
periods of stability; hence, management's major job involves detecting discontinuities as early as possible and adapting their strategies to meet those discontinuities most successfully. When
minor discontinuities occur, managers should make minimal
changes to historically successful strategies and minimize disruptions
to the companies' smooth functioning. When major discontinuities
occur, managers should decide upon the best strategies to move
quickly from discontinuity to stability to maximize profits once
again.

Knowing the business

Mintzberg contended that the best planning and implementation of plans occur when management knows the business of its companies inside and out. This stipulation holds especially true for the hands' activities in strategic planning. Hands' knowledge arises through responsibility for line activities on a day-to-day basis. Through managing line activities, managers learn the different nuances, potential problems and synergies that can arise when different functions of the companies conduct business and interact.

Managing patterns

Mintzberg indicated that managers can most efficiently and profitably manage periods of stability by developing and recognizing patterns. In particular, managers must recognize the patterns that emerge in their companies' environments and business activities. Additionally, managers must develop behavioral patterns to manipulate efficiently the companies' controllable variables and to influence effectively the environmental patterns. In effect, managers must manage the relevant patterns so that they interact and mesh together optimally.

Reconciling change and continuity

According to Mintzberg, managers' primary functions involve reconciling changes and continuities. In uncertain times, managers should not manage change but rather work through the discontinuities as quickly as possible to re-establish stability. During periods of change, profits appear uncertain and highly variable, making transitions to periods of stability desirable where profits assume more certainty.

Earlier in the section, we described Mintzberg's concept of planning with minds. Mintzberg developed his alternate concept of planning with hands through observing his wife, a professional potter, make her pottery. She planned with the mind, selecting the correct amount and type of clay for her pottery and producing them on her pottery wheel. Sometimes he noted that the figure that resulted was not one she had planned. While working, she often found that miscalculations, fresh insights, whims or instincts, influenced her to produce something different for her market. She operated instinctively so that her ability to innovate appeared to draw on her profound, ingrained knowledge of her craft and her market. The resultant product incorporated her strategy. She generated her strategy purposefully or in reaction to unexpected developments, but could do so intuitively only because of her profound knowledge of her craft, business, and market. She had acquired her profound knowledge through her experience in making and selling her product: basically, she had line-management experience.

Line management's knowledge and experience differ significantly from that of staff. Line management and personnel acquire all the necessary components and raw materials to produce the companies' products. They deal with the nuances of translating R&D prototypes for production lines; they work to manufacture their products in the most efficient way possible given the specific capital equipment and personnel the companies possess. They develop the logistical and distribution channels that move the products to market; and finally, they interact daily with customers and their problems. By facing and dealing with routine problems, line management and personnel develop instinctive understandings of the requirements for success in their industries and markets; their understandings for success differ significantly, and often have richer more-textured tones, than those that staff personnel develop through their analyses.

Mintzberg (1985), and Mintzberg and Waters (1987) also categorized strategic plans as directed or emergent. Directed strategic plans develop through the classical strategic planning processes that we discussed earlier in this section. Emergent strategic plans evolve from the collective, behavioral patterns of companies' employees as they react to environmental stimuli. When crafting strategy, they argue, for the best planning, managers need both directed and emergent strategic planning.

Emergent strategic plans develop through the management groups' collective experiences and the companies' learned business behaviors. Mintzberg described the process as a 'bubbling up' of strategic plans from the lower levels of management to higher levels: line managers react to problems they face in their business activities which the company's official strategic or operational plans either ignore or cannot solve.

Mintzberg also noted that strategic planning through a bubbling-up process can have competitive dimensions. As different personnel probably encounter the same or similar problems, the individuals will probably develop ranges of solutions from slight variations on the same theme to entirely different solutions for solving the immediate problems. When the company faces minor discontinuities, these local adaptations generally maintain the company's profitability without senior managers' attention. However, when the company faces major discontinuities, the local adaptations bubble upwards towards senior managers; the adaptations compete for senior managers' attention to be incorporated into, or to form the basis of, the company's new primary strategic postures – their attempts to re-attain stability.

We believe that Mintzberg's conceptualization of crafting strategy best describes and explains the strategic management of the Overseas Chinese. In the balance of the chapter, we will demonstrate the similarities between Mintzberg's concepts and the management practices of the Overseas Chinese.

A summary of Overseas Chinese management practices

We present here a short summary of the Overseas Chinese management practices that we have delineated in detail in the previous chapters. The Overseas Chinese strategic planning methods emphasize line management through depending on soft data and on intimate, intuitive understandings of their businesses and the environments. As Haley and Tan described (1996), their managers disdain the separation of planning and doing. These tendencies allow Overseas Chinese companies to employ and to use fewer staff than Western companies. For example, Hong Kong companies' average sizes shrank by 59 percent from 1954 to 1984, although their operations expanded significantly during this period (Redding, 1986).

Haley and Tan (1996) also noted five practices of Overseas Chinese management, namely:

- Hands-on experience
- Transfers of knowledge across businesses
- Qualitative information
- Holistic information processing
- Action-driven decision-making

Enormous similarities in virtually every aspect of strategic planning appear when we compare the management practices of the Overseas Chinese with the conceptualization of strategic planning developed by Mintzberg and his colleagues. In the next section we elaborate on these similarities for a fresh understanding of the New Asian Emperors' strategic behaviors.

The Overseas Chinese and crafting strategy

Mintzberg's theoretical constructs seem to capture many facets of the Overseas Chinese networks' strategic planning processes and modes (Haley, G. T., 1997). Mintzberg's observation that the best strategic plans incorporate directed and emergent elements – and that strategic plans often evolve from the collective, behavioral patterns of companies' employees (1985, 1987, 1994) as they react to environmental stimuli, form apt descriptors for the New Asian Emperors' strategic plans.

Because of their founders' characteristics, emergent strategic planning appears prevalent among the Overseas Chinese companies. Haley and Tan (1996) described how the founders of most of the Overseas Chinese companies, though highly intelligent, had little formal education and even less management education. Hence their decision-making evolved within a different perspective of what constitutes acceptable data than most Western managers have. Overseas Chinese managers used data drawn from their experiences, advice from trusted friends, and their perceptions of the situations.

With soft data, strategy emerges from the Overseas Chinese managers' interactions with their environments. A good example occurred when (noted in the previous chapter) the Wuthelam Group's senior executive saw a property development in receivership and immediately reacted based on his knowledge and experience of the industry. For a typical Overseas Chinese company, news, rumors or insider information will reach an executive and create interest. The executive will then seek out confirming evidence and gauge available resources. The executive will analyze the situation, make and implement decisions. As the implementation proceeds, further information will become available and the executive's strategy will emerge and be fleshed out; he or she will either stand firm, continue along the same path, or make the strategic alterations deemed necessary. The strategies which the company follows will emerge from the executive's and the company's learned business behaviors and their increasing collection of knowledge dealing with the specific situation of the company's investment. Thus, as Wuthelam Group's top managers became more comfortable with their initial strike into New Zealand property development, they decided to expand their initial NZ$17 million investment into one which eventually exceeded NZ$1 billion.

If the executives feel the need for a strategic partner, the company will seek one out. Though major Overseas Chinese companies have family bases, and major individual companies form significant conglomerates, potential partners within the Overseas Chinese networks will base their decisions largely on the confidence and trust they have in the proposing executives' judgment and managerial abilities. When the strategy moves from one for a single company into one adopted by the company's network of associates, it resembles Mintzberg's bubbling-up process of strategy development. While this bubbling-up process occurs on an intra-company basis in most companies, within the Overseas Chinese networks, it regularly occurs on a supra-company basis.

The Overseas Chinese and Mintzberg's four activities

Detecting discontinuities and qualitative data – Mintzberg specified detecting discontinuities as the essence of strategic planning; Haley and Tan (1996) discerned this process when analyzing how Overseas Chinese managers use contacts within local governments and communities as primary sources of data. Through their web of associates, the Overseas Chinese managers determine potential changes in government policy or business, social and economic environments that can cause discontinuities and force divestment or changes of business strategies. United Overseas Bank's Wee Cho Yaw alluded to detecting discontinuities when he told us, 'market information is often exchanged in social settings'. Managers discussed and analyzed information in these social gatherings to determine the state of affairs and to ascertain if any changes would affect their businesses. The Overseas Chinese businessmen's trust in each other had evolved over years of friendship and business dealings; Wee and his associates formed a network among themselves for gathering and disseminating information.

Knowing the business and hands-on experience – knowing the business constitutes another of Mintzberg's characteristics and translates directly into the hands-on experience identified by Haley and Tan (1996). Mintzberg emphasized that managers must have an intimate knowledge of their business – its markets, its products, its distribution and logistical systems, its production processes, and its operations; line management experiences provide excellent avenues to garner this intimate knowledge. Overseas Chinese managers emphasize active, intimate participation in all the important aspects of their companies' activities and product/markets. They also stress getting one's hands dirty in the companies' operations – and the need

---

Wee Cho Yaw – United Overseas Bank: banker on the make

Wee Cho Yaw, chairman of United Overseas Bank Group (UOB), unlike the other executives profiled, is not the founder of his company and does not see himself as an entrepreneur. As a second-generation manager, he took over his father's bank and expanded it into one of Singapore's 'Big Four' banks, alongside Overseas Chinese Banking Corporation, Development Bank of Singapore and Overseas Union Bank.

Over the years, Wee aggressively pursued a policy of acquisition, diversification, and international expansion. Today, the UOB Group is more than a banking and financial services company; it has interests in property development, hotel

---

management, trading, manufacturing, and the travel industry in many parts of the world.

UOB's status as a leading bank in the region is partly due to an innovative and aggressive marketing and expansion strategy, and partly to a series of acquisitions. In 1971, it took over Chung Khiaw Bank, then in succession through 1987, Lee Wah Bank, Far Eastern Bank, and Industrial Commercial Bank. With the banking market saturated in Singapore, UOB has plans to push its operations further into the region. Wee said, 'The banks can't grow very much in Singapore. We have to move out and go regional, perhaps even global' (*Asian Business*, December, 1995, p. 55).

Wee is confident about China, saying, 'We speak the same language. Some 70 percent of Singapore's population is Chinese, and virtually all the first generation hail from China. There are still a lot of connections' (*Asian Business*, December, 1995, p. 59). With personal contacts, confidence and trust, UOB has responded to the Singaporean government's investment into China by opening up offices there. Wee looks at China as a medium- to long-term investment situation.

The old Chinese saying goes, 'Fortune does not last three generations'; however, the Wee family's fortune has grown from a small bank to a large, diversified company. The third generation has reached the stature of senior management, and shows no sign of diminishing. Together with a solid team of high-caliber professional managers, many recruited from top international banks, the third generation represented by Wee's son, Wee Ee Cheong, is starting to take charge of operations.

Like all truly successful Chinese businessmen, Wee Cho Yaw is a prominent Chinese leader in his home country, Singapore. He is involved in several civic organizations, and on the boards of many other business and social organizations. As the honorary president of the Singapore Chamber of Commerce and Industry and president of the Singapore Hokkien Huay Kuan, Wee plays the role of a Chinese community elder. Increasingly, the day-to-day running of his business is being passed over to the third generation. As his son, Wee Ee Cheong, said, 'the key job is to spot talents and to bring them into the bank'. Clearly, preparation for the fourth generation to take over is under way.

to deal with more than descriptive statistics. A quote from a Singaporean entrepreneur, Aw Kim Chen, speaking about the start up of his rubber manufacturing business, indicates this characteristic clearly (Chan and Chiang, 1994):

> I alone transacted business with the foreign countries. I also dealt with the local businessmen. I did the purchasing myself. I also took charge of the technical aspects of the factory, putting to use the rubber-processing techniques which I had learnt when I was working in the Lam Aik Rubber Factory.

As the above quote reveals, Aw Kim Chen got intrinsically involved in every aspect of his business. His experiences gave him the intimate, incisive knowledge of his business which forms the keystone to the intuitive decision-making that distinguishes the Overseas Chinese. Also, only small companies allow such intrinsic, intimate involvement in all aspects of their business – a factor that the Overseas Chinese recognize in their organizational structures. Most Overseas Chinese businesses remain relatively small; over time, the total size of all a family's businesses may add up to a large conglomerate. Additionally, when Overseas Chinese companies grow beyond any individual's abilities to undertake all of Aw's activities, employees' duties change: Owners concentrate on managerial, financial and investment decisions; trusted subordinates on the production floor concentrate on manufacturing, purchasing and sales.

Managing patterns and holistic information processing – Mintzberg argued that business strategists' primary duties included perceiving and managing the emerging patterns of companies' operations and markets. Haley and Tan (1996) similarly identified managing patterns in the holistic information processing of the Overseas Chinese. In both instances, the strategists rely on perceptions, not on hard data or on collective manifestations of it that could display significant distortions. These perceptions of holistic data, viewed as patterns, lead the strategists to infer the companies' present and future relationships with its internal and external environments; the perceptions also present avenues to manage effectively the companies' resources and to optimize present and future benefits. Overseas Chinese managers use networks to obtain the necessary perceptions about their business, market environments and potential coming changes; these views collectively, form the patterns that they manage.

Li & Fung – traders extraordinaires

Most Overseas Chinese companies started as trading companies. As they grew, they diversified into other businesses; many moved away from trading. Over the last two decades the trading business has become one of the most difficult and competitive industries in Asia. Even the old, huge, traditional European trading companies such as Inchcape and East Asiatic have suffered. Few have been able to develop value-added activities which would justify their existence. Li & Fung is the exception. Not only has it survived, it has been able to provide value-added services to its associates in the distribution channel.

Li & Fung was founded about 90 years ago by the grandfather of its present chairman, Victor Fung. Hong Kong's boom days of the 1960s and 1970s, created by its low-cost manufacturing base, also benefited Li & Fung. Rapidly increasing exports and the constant need for brokering between US buyers and Hong Kong manufacturers created a prosperous niche for Li & Fung. The company went public in 1973 and in 1995 made headlines when it purchased Inchcape Buying Service (IBS), its major rival, from parent company, Inchcape, a British conglomerate.

Victor Fung holds a PhD in business economics from Harvard University. He serves as the highly visible chairman of one of Hong Kong's highest profile agencies, the Hong Kong Trade Development Council, and has won wide acclaim for both his business acumen and public service to Hong Kong.

He and brother William have worked hard to move Li & Fung up the value chain at a time when profit margins were being squeezed and most trading companies were having trouble just surviving. The growing sophistication of both buyers and sellers is threatening to eliminate altogether trading houses as intermediaries. Rather than fleeing the industry, Li & Fung has responded by serving both their upstream and downstream customers. They have become involved in their customers' design, marketing and planning of products at one end; and in the packaging shipping and distribution of those products at the other end.

Victor Fung said that, 'A product costs US$1.00 when it comes out of the factory in Asia. By the time it gets to the retail shelves in the US it is going to cost US$4.00. The secret is to try to earn a bigger share of that 4:1 mark-up' (*Asian Business*, March, 1996, p. 70).

Li & Fung has survived and prospered by seeing opportunities and value where others did not, and integrating modern business concepts into an ancient business.

Haley and Tan (1996) also detected how the Overseas Chinese manage patterns in the transfer of knowledge. They identified how Overseas Chinese managers extrapolate what they have learned and experienced in one product/market to different, unrelated product/markets. By considering similarities and dissimilarities of the different product/markets, the managers are also considering similarities and dissimilarities in the patterns of behavior and requirements for success in the venues. These similarities are the factors which help turn a 'different egg' into a 'new opportunity', as the long-time, senior executive from Wuthelam Group described to us.

Reconciling change and continuity and the networks – Mintzberg argued that in order to optimize a company's performance, the strategist must encourage the emergence of some patterns, and delay, or even prevent the emergence of other patterns – thereby reconciling change and continuity. Through their web of associates, most especially local-government associates, the Overseas Chinese managers seek information – and where possible, also pursue preferential treatment, and lobby for or against the promulgation of laws, regulations, and privileged positions within desired markets and industries. In this fashion, Overseas Chinese managers strive to enhance patterns of change and continuity that enhance their strengths and minimize their weaknesses.

The Overseas Chinese have proven enormously successful in their lobbying efforts, often building monopolies in strategic Southeast Asian industries through key governmental contacts and connections. New Asian Emperor, Robert Kuok, has had great success in this arena. In 1959 he founded Malaysian Sugar Manufacturing. At the time Malaysia had no sugar plantations but Kuok planted 2,600 hectares in a partnership with the government's Federal Land Development Authority. Thus, Kuok secured a near-monopoly of Malaysia's sugar market. In 1964, he opened his first sugar refinery. When he moved to Indonesia in the mid-1970s he achieved dominance of the Indonesian sugar market through similar means. Kuok's long-term investments in Malaysia and other Southeast Asian countries secured his reputation. Governments in the region learned that they could trust him to work for national as well as personal advantage. An executive with Kuok's flagship Malaysian company, Perlis Plantations, succinctly explains Kuok's special relations with the Malaysian government: 'We did our national service' (*Asia, Inc.*, December, 1994). We should note here that many in the West disparagingly refer to this system as crony capitalism; yet, it prevails across Asia, including non-Chinese groups such as the Japanese and the Koreans.

The Overseas Chinese and their core competencies

The Overseas Chinese have tended to follow conglomerate diversification. In an earlier chapter we highlighted the important characteristics that distinguish successful, local companies operating in South and Southeast Asia, which we now summarize:

- The companies appear highly diversified; often, they undertake unrelated diversification, contravening mainstream theoretical notions.
- The companies have good relationships with the often enormous, public sectors in these countries.
- The companies have very strong familial and informal networks.
- Managers tend to use subjective information as inputs to decision-making.

The Salim Group of Indonesia, the largest of the Overseas Chinese companies, demonstrates the above characteristics in the following fashion (East Asia Analytical Unit, 1995; Kohut and Cheng, 1996).

- Salim has interests in cement, processed foods, flour milling, steel, banking, real estate, investments, pharmaceuticals, information technology, chemicals, shipping, general manufacturing, and vehicle assembly.

- Salim's close ties to the government in its home base of Indonesia are shown by its government contracts for flour milling (at an estimated fee of 300 percent of world prices), its sharing exclusive rights to import cloves into Indonesia with one other company, and the many Salim companies that have the government as a minority shareholder.
- Salim has close ties, as manifested by joint ventures, management contracts and strategic alliances with Indonesia's Lippo Group, Ciputra Group, Sinar Mas Group, Barito Group, and Ongko Group, Malaysia's Robert Kuok, Taiwan's Koo family, and Thailand's Sophanpanich family, among others.

The above practices would seem to run contrary to Prahalad and Hamel's (1990) tenets on developing one's core competency, but they do not. While the Overseas Chinese companies have pursued conglomerate diversification, they have instinctively developed, nurtured and protected their core competencies:

- their decision-making styles
- their control over information
- and their networks.

First, many attribute the rapid growth of the Overseas Chinese businesses in Southeast Asia to their **decision-making style**, especially their speed of decision-making (Chu and MacMurray, 1993). This speed, and their dominant control of information (another core competency), facilitate Overseas Chinese efforts to seize business opportunities before competitors sense they exist (Redding, 1986; Haley and Tan, 1996).

The Overseas Chinese decision-making style (that we detailed in Chapter Four) provides them with access to various markets (a requirement for a core competency) with scant data for making analytical decisions. The decision-making style also allows them to take advantages of opportunities such as scarce goods and services, and transfer them to customers, thereby providing the customers with benefits (another requirement for a core competency). Finally, competitors have difficulties imitating this decision-making style (a third requirement for a core competency) – especially the multinationals that depend on decision techniques better suited for industrialized markets; and local businessmen that lack the

Overseas Chinese managers' hands-on knowledge and business experiences.

Second, the Overseas Chinese control over the rich information they obtain through their networks, a rare commodity in non-governmental circles, also displays all the characteristics of a core competency. The Overseas Chinese managers notably control specialized business information – much of which is considered 'insider information' in the West. The Overseas Chinese prosper and produce goods in the informational void that they create and perpetuate. Their information arbitrage provides potential benefits to customers and competitors have difficulties imitating it. The New Asian Emperors' region-wide, and increasingly world-wide, business activities endorse their access to a variety of markets. We have indicated the Salim's group's diversity; other examples of Overseas Chinese conglomerate diversification abound. Thailand's Chearavanont Family (CP Group) went from poultry farming into real estate, and telecommunications; the Philippines' Lucio Tan is involved in beer, tobacco, banking and diversified investments; and, in previous chapters, we have sketched the extremely varied investments of Malaysia's Robert Kuok. The Overseas Chinese generally exhibit intense privacy, jealously maintaining secrecy over the sources of information that guide their investments.

New Asian Emperor, Robert Kuok, has built a legendary reputation for contributing to and maintaining the informational void in South and Southeast Asia. A few years ago, a leading international investigative agency took an in-depth look at the Kuok Group of companies. After an intensive research effort that spanned six countries, the agency produced a detailed report on the companies' operations, and almost nothing about its management strategies. However, its conclusions about Robert Kuok whose management acumen binds the companies and provides their focus were startling:

Name:	Robert Kuok
Political affiliation:	unknown
Adversaries:	none identified
Litigation:	nothing known
Ambitions:	not known

For a man whose business empire stretches from Chile to China and who counts among his friends and partners some of Asia's most powerful politicians and tycoons, Kuok has a remarkable ability to divulge nothing. Over a 50-year career, Kuok has made secrecy both his trademark and his principal asset. He has maintained a wall of secrecy even between himself and the 10 public companies he controls. Five of the listed companies represent the Shangri-La chain and other property investments. They own the bricks and mortar of 27 Shangri-La hotels and resorts around the region; but, the management of the hotels – the factor that makes them successful and the area where Kuok's business acumen really counts – remains in the hands of his private company, Shangri-La International Hotel Management. Similar arrangements exist for Kuala Lumpur listed Federal Flour Mills Bhd, and Perlis Plantations Bhd, through which many of Kuok's edible oil and sugar plantations have been listed. The quoted companies allow the public to buy into Kuok's production and refining businesses; but his commodity trading, the business on which his reputation rests, is almost all in the hands of private companies.

Finally, for the Overseas Chinese **their networks** provide a core competency. The networks provide potential access to various markets, as demonstrated through the Overseas Chinese ethnic, governmental and familial contacts. Competitors lack the web of contacts that the Overseas Chinese possess through their networks; consequently, most potential, independent local competitors fail to grow large enough to challenge them in the region. Competitors also cannot replicate these textured networks (described in earlier chapters).

The wide networks that the Overseas Chinese use to promote their connections are referred to in Mandarin Chinese as *guanxi* or influential connections. The practice of *guanxi* leads to a high degree of reliance on trust. *Guanxi*'s role also helps to explain why the Overseas Chinese have tended to keep their individual investments in China small or medium-sized. By doing so they can take advantage of their connections with local officials who do not have to submit projects to Beijing for state approval unless they exceed US$30 million.

For the New Asian Emperors, the 'complex harmonization of individual technologies and production skills' that Prahalad and Hamel (1990, p. 84) identified has led to their strategic dominance of Southeast and East Asian business environments. As indicated in previous chapters, neither local competitors nor foreign multinationals can challenge or duplicate the Overseas Chinese abilities to make

Charoen Pokphand Group – the classic network company

Charoen Pokphand Group (CP) is probably one of the most diversified conglomerates in the Overseas Chinese business world, and many consider it the classic Overseas Chinese network company. CP was founded in 1921 by two brothers who emigrated from China to Bangkok, Thailand. The first business they entered was seed trading. Today, agriculture is still a core business for the group, but it has diverse interests. The breadth of CP's business is phenomenal: it operates fast food chains, has a retailing chain of superstores called Lotus (modelled after Wal-mart), owns Wholesalers called Makro, and runs the second largest 7–11 franchise in the world after Japan. It produces PVC and motorcycles, has a chain of gas stations, breeds chickens, brews beer, manages real estate and has entered the telecommunications and petrochemicals industries.

CP's chairman, Dhanin Chearavanont, manages hundreds of companies through a large number of partnerships, and is considered a visionary leader among the Overseas Chinese. The ability to manage effectively large numbers of relationships, some of which come into conflict with one another, is considered his greatest skill. He has used his many strategic alliances, joint ventures and partnerships to both expand his company and to acquire technology and know-how from the West.

CP's growth has stemmed from its management's understanding of Asian culture. It often enters a project through low bids, sometimes willing to accept losses in order to obtain a foothold or establish a crucial new relationship.

To handle the CP Group's extreme diversity, subsidiaries are largely autonomous; headquarters basically acts as a co-ordinator of financial resources.

CP is reputed to be the single largest foreign investor in China, though the size and nature of its investments are somewhat unclear. We do know that CP Group entered China in 1979 and now has over 100 joint venture companies in China. It is one of the few companies with substantial investments in China's agricultural interior provinces.

Continuing in its unique way, in recent years, CP group has

> moved away from partnerships and joint ventures with major Western and Overseas Chinese companies in their Chinese investments, and has sought to bring smaller Thai companies into projects. So far, CP has US$1 billion in these projects with small companies.

effective strategic decisions, through their networks, in the informational void they maintain.

Some final considerations

Ghosh and Chan (1994), in their study of strategic planning behaviors among companies in Singapore and Malaysia, classified their planning activities as ad hoc and reactive. The only important, market-related factor that they found centered on the 'CEO's personal knowledge of market', which was the fourth most-important contributing factor to success in planning. Their findings reflect the Overseas Chinese highly centralized decision-making (Redding, 1986; Haley and Tan, 1996): specifically, the 'CEO's personal knowledge' of the market assumes importance, not the company's or the marketing manager's.

With this chapter we conclude the book's strategic analysis section. In our final section we will discuss the implications of the strategic management style of the Overseas Chinese. While the Overseas Chinese possess tremendous competitive advantages, they also possess significant competitive disadvantages which will be discussed in the implications section that follows.

Part Three

The Implications for Business

Chapter Six

Competitive Implications of the Overseas Chinese:

doing business with the New Asian emperors

> 'Remember that you are responsible to your ancestors, not just to yourself. Our ancestors are not honored by compromise; they are honored by responsible behavior and hard work.'
>
> Tan Suang U. To his son in Batan, quoted in Tan, 1991, p. 205

Introduction

The quote above exemplifies the Overseas Chinese work ethic within their authoritarian Confucian culture of compromise. We have studied a large portion of the business literature on the Overseas Chinese, discussed our ideas with many of the community's patriarchs (including some of the New Asian Emperors), advised many of their companies and their competitors, and studied them for several years. In our final chapter, we synthesize our findings to discuss the implications of the Overseas Chinese strategic planning styles and delineate their comparative advantages and disadvantages. We will also discuss the advantages and disadvantages of competing against or co-operating with the Overseas Chinese.

First, we discuss the competitive advantages and disadvantages of the Overseas Chinese manner of doing business. Next, we elaborate on the implications that the Overseas Chinese decision-making style has for the conduct of business in Southeast Asia. Beginning with a fairly general discussion, we move to specific areas of strategic management including human resource management, product management, and distribution management. Finally, we close with short discussions of the future influence of the Overseas Chinese on practice and research.

The competitive advantages of the Overseas Chinese

Many opinions exist on the competitive advantages of the Overseas Chinese. Drawing on the core competencies that we identified in the previous chapter, we argue that the following factors provide the Overseas Chinese with competitive advantages in their business dealings in Southeast and East Asia:

- speed
- knowledge
- *guanxi*.

Speed

Their speed of decision and action flows from their decision-making style, a core competency of the Overseas Chinese that we previously identified. Many Western observers note speed as the primary competitive advantage of the Overseas Chinese. When asked about their greatest competitive advantage, many of the Overseas Chinese will also mention speed. When interviewed for this book, Stan Shih of Acer Computers told us, 'We believe in doing things quickly', and 'We implement and change things quickly. It's all implementation in the market place'.

Both Western and Overseas Chinese decision-making styles accept the existence of uncertainty, and try to minimize that uncertainty. However, Western strategic decision-making depends heavily on quantifiable and measurable data. Western managers are often stymied when they confront an environment that does not provide the data that they require and to which they are accustomed, thus delaying strategic decisions for many Western companies. The Overseas Chinese managers can arrive quickly at strategic decisions with a minimum of information and primarily through the use of subjective data, thus speeding strategic decisions for their companies. Moreover, many strategic decisions of Western companies go through levels of hierarchy that do not exist in Overseas Chinese companies. Consequently, the Overseas Chinese companies have a nimbleness that most major Western companies envy.

Knowledge

Their knowledge stems from their control of information, a core competency of the Overseas Chinese that we previously identified. The Overseas Chinese have recognized their competitive advantage and actively sought to monopolize sources of special market and business information. Historically, their manner of conducting business has involved developing their sources of information to the greatest extent possible. Their networking provides their market research, and their talks with friends and sifting of their experiences serve as their analysis. Combined, these two activities provide the Overseas Chinese with the inputs and analysis necessary for informed decision-making. The Overseas Chinese, however, can create and maintain a monopoly over this knowledge relatively easily.

The Overseas Chinese create their competitive advantages in market and business information in two ways. First, they practice an exclusionary style of business. This statement does not mean that all the Overseas Chinese networks exclude non-Chinese. Contrary to popular opinion, the Overseas Chinese do have people of other nationalities in their networks and their companies' inner circles. Indeed, close inspection of the Overseas Chinese networks and companies in Southeast Asia will indicate that both include many non-Chinese members. Like other business people, the Overseas Chinese look for trustworthy, upright, hard working, honest, loyal individuals that possess talents needed by their circles of friends and associates. However, the Overseas Chinese style of business excludes those people who are not associates from possessing the same advantages that the Overseas Chinese and their associates have. Competitors and non-associates find that they simply cannot obtain the quality and quantity of knowledge in order to compete on more equal footings.

Second, the Overseas Chinese maintain a competitive advantage in knowledge through inaction. If the more economically advanced Southeast Asian countries' business communities desired freer and greater availability of market and business information, they would lobby their governments and probably obtain its release. Indeed, the Southeast Asian governments do provide data for the markets: however, at least two types of data exist – data which are freely available and therefore of little competitive consequence; and 'special data'. Various Southeast Asian networks generally enjoy exclusive access to the special data. As these networks prefer to maintain their monopoly over the local markets' special data, they do not lobby their governments for level playing fields.

Guanxi

Guanxi (a Mandarin term, with no exact English translation, which includes concepts of trust and the ability and knowledge of how to present uprightness to build relationships) stems from their networks, a core competency of the Overseas Chinese that we previously identified. *Guanxi* also builds networks. The ability to generate trust, and to judge who among others is worthy of trust, constitutes a true competitive advantage for the Overseas Chinese in Southeast Asia. Though Westerners obviously have the ability to judge others and to generate trust among others, this aspect of doing business forms one of the most culturally specific aspects imaginable.

Guanxi provides Overseas Chinese with an important competitive advantage over Western companies: discrepancy in the availability of information between Western companies and Overseas Chinese companies. Most Western companies entering Southeast Asia are large, publicly held companies and information about their operations and strategies is freely available. If a company develops an exemplary reputation, that becomes freely available knowledge. Alternatively, if a company develops a reputation for having difficulties in its dealings with Asian partners and customers, that also becomes freely available knowledge or knowledge that the networks can obtain through their contacts.

Conversely, as we indicated in the previous chapter, most people without local contacts have difficulty obtaining knowledge on the Overseas Chinese companies. Most Overseas Chinese companies constitute closely held companies about which information is not widely available or published, especially in Western circles. Many Westerners have no knowledge of the Asia-based publications or sources that may provide valuable sources of information or strategic leads. Due to the closely guarded privacy of most Overseas Chinese businessmen, and their proclivity to share information only among their own networks of friends and associates, most Overseas Chinese businessmen will not divulge information about local markets or business situations to strangers. Trust usually develops through years of socializing and doing business with people. Also, Overseas Chinese generally judge individuals, not companies; they direct their loyalty and trust accordingly towards individuals rather than companies. We next discuss some of their attendant competitive disadvantages.

The competitive disadvantages of the Overseas Chinese

As Lao Tzu would have recognized, many of the competitive disadvantages of the Overseas Chinese stem from their competitive advantages. The disadvantages that we perceive them to have are the following:

- home turf only
- susceptibility to be blind-sided

- proprietary capabilities
- family limits.

Home turf only

Their home turf only disadvantage stems from their control of information, a core competency of the Overseas Chinese that we previously identified. In some industries, the Overseas Chinese appear extremely competitive regardless of where they operate. For example, the Overseas Chinese have proven extremely successful in property development and the hotel and resort investments that they make. However, the Overseas Chinese frequently have trouble when they move into manufacturing industries. For example, New Asian Emperor, Li Kai Shang, called Superman in Hong Kong for his skills in manipulating the system, has failed badly in two mid-1980s forays into Western markets (Cheng and Vriens, 1996/97): In Canada, he bought Husky Oil Ltd and had to swallow losses of US$183 million before his acquisition finally turned a dollar in 1993; and, in Britain, his company, Hutchison, set up a cordless-phone operation called Rabbit that flopped and again had to swallow losses of US$183 million before it cut the line. Similarly, Creative Technology, with 60 percent market share worldwide in the sound card market has historically done poorly in the US market.

The Overseas Chinese companies often fail in the West because they depend upon an intimate knowledge of both their business and their markets for their decisions. Consequently, the Overseas Chinese managers come to expect, and to depend on, an advantage in the quantity and quality of strategic information. When they leave their home markets, they lose their access to this special business information. Thus, historically, they have done poorly away from their home turfs and have not posed serious threats to move into Western multinationals' home markets as the Japanese companies did. However, Western companies can no longer depend upon this advantage. The founding generations of Overseas Chinese businessmen are increasingly retiring and handing over the reins to their heirs. Unlike past generations, these heirs have training in the traditional business practices of the Overseas Chinese, and from the best business schools of the West. Many have significant experience in

China and the Overseas Chinese – or reaching out through the networks

Thousands of business delegations now leave China each year to contact local ethnic Chinese communities, and local Chinese Chambers of Commerce, across the Asia Pacific, in their quest for investments for their home areas in China. The *hua qiao* or Overseas Chinese community now constitutes the single biggest group of investors in China. Through family/clan, regional and dialect ties, the Overseas Chinese have created an empire without borders that generates an estimated GDP of around US$450 billion – only fractionally less than that of mainland China. Now, some of that money is pouring back into the mainland. Traditionally, Overseas Chinese have preferred to do business with people of their own dialect or clan. In Malaysia, on the booming Penang waterfront, seven old piers represent the different clan-based *gongsi* (syndicates) that used to trade exclusively with their own kind. Typically, New Asian Emperor, Li Kai Shang, who was born in 1928 in the sleepy city of Chaozhou (Chiuchow in Cantonese) in southeast Guangdong, has made many financial investments and commitments to his ancestral region including US$13 million to various Chaozhou charities and US$152 million for the founding of Shantou University in the nearby city of Shantou. 'I'm a Chiuchow person', Li told friends in China in the early 1990s, 'I'll earn money elsewhere and bring it back home'. Many delegations originate from specific parts of China and frequently attempt to contact their former compatriots now living abroad. For example, in 1994, a business delegation from Fuzhou in Fujian province visited the timber and logging city of Sibu in Malaysia's Sarawak. Sibu has a high concentration of Overseas Chinese who originate from Fuzhou. The New Asian Emperors have not forgotten home.

Western multinationals and have been prepared to live and to conduct business in both worlds. Many of the heirs appear to be formidable opponents as we discuss in later sections.

Susceptibility to blind-siding

Their susceptibility to blind-siding stems from their networks, a core competency of the Overseas Chinese that we previously identified. Any trust-based system such as the Overseas Chinese networks is susceptible to blind-siding. Though trust provides enormous economic benefits (Fukuyama, 1995), it does expose those employing it as a primary competitive tool to significant losses. The collapse of Peregrine Investments' Holdings presents an example of blind-siding. Peregrine was an Asian high flier which, in 10 years, grew to be the largest home-grown investment house in Asia. Peregrine's collapse came after the Indonesian rupiah was allowed to float and became seriously devalued. Because of the devaluation, a major Indonesian debtor, Steady Safe, could not repay the US$260 million bridge loan it owed to Peregrine. Peregrine has been unable to reclaim a single cent of the loan; and, investigators have been unable to determine what actually happened to the US$260 million. Given the economic difficulties in Indonesia, one can comprehend that Steady Safe's bond issue and loan went sour (despite the Suharto family's support); however, the complete disappearance without a trace of US$260 million clearly indicates a breakdown in the trust-based relationships of the Overseas Chinese. As the networks draw so completely on trust, any significant trend towards blind-siding can bring the system crashing down.

Poor proprietary capabilities

Their poor proprietary capabilities stem from the sometimes reactive natures of their strategic decision-making style. As we indicated in the previous chapter, many have noted (Ghosh and Chan, 1994) that the average Overseas Chinese company appears reactive. This characteristic holds true for the average Western company too. However, the major Western multinationals have only recently begun to sell their products in Overseas Chinese companies' home markets; and though relatively new to the environment and, in many instances struggling, Western multinationals have the brand-name recognition and technological prowess that many Overseas Chinese companies lack. The Overseas Chinese companies' reactive natures may hinder them from aggressively building their names and developing their technologies. Stan Shih of Acer recognized this major potential problem when he said in an interview, 'Branding is natural to an American company but is unusual in this part of the world' (*Business Times*, 17 October, 1997): few Overseas Chinese companies are struggling to build their brand equity within the region as fiercely as Acer.

McDonald's constitutes the best-known restaurant in Asia; Coke and Pepsi form the best-known soft drinks. Procter & Gamble already holds a 60 percent market share in China's shampoo market – even at three times the price of local products. The US, European and Japanese giants of Procter & Gamble, Unilever and Kao have started waging their battle of the detergents (*The Economist*, 9 March, 1996). The failure of many of the Overseas Chinese companies to establish brand recognition or loyalty, or to exercise a technological edge, may seriously prevent their establishing market niches once the Japanese and Western consumer-product companies move into Southeast Asia in full force.

Family limits

The family limits on Overseas Chinese companies originate from the Chinese business approximating the Chinese family. Traditionally, when the family can no longer provide the skills necessary, an Overseas Chinese company reaches the limits of its growth, and in fact often begins to decline. In actuality, non-family members can become, for all practical purposes, parts of the family by showing their worth within the company's business, so the limitation is not as restrictive as it initially may seem. However, once a company grows beyond the size where it can be run as a family, and once one authoritarian patriarch can no longer efficiently centralize decision-making within himself, the family has to make changes in how they run their business.

Several Overseas Chinese companies have already encountered the problem of family limits, and many companies have successfully adapted. Though, when the emperors pass on or retire, the succession period will pose a significant threat to many of the great Overseas Chinese empires. Some companies appear to be making the transition smoothly, such as United Overseas Bank, Wuthelam Group of Singapore, and Hutchison Whampoa/Cheung Kong Holdings of Hong Kong; but for others, such as Malaysia's Kerry Group, the succession promises difficulties. The Wanglee's of Thailand have shown that despite the biting Chinese prophecy of wealth not surviving to the third generations, successful successions can occur.

General implications for multinationals

In Southeast and East Asia, multinationals serve markets about which little information and market research are available. To compete successfully, multinationals from the industrialized economies must offset the Overseas Chinese competitive advantage in knowledge, even if the multinational is seeking a local partner (Haley and Haley, 1997). The multinationals must determine which markets they aim to serve. While information is lacking, it does exist for the multinationals; their managers must dredge it up, collate and analyse it, seek out both hard data and subjective, the most up-to-date data and historical. Western managers must treat research as an investment that will produce substantial returns; they should remember that those returns come both in the form of earning future profits and avoiding future losses.

The multinationals can use the data they gather to prioritize potential product/markets and to identify the major players and influences in them. They can determine which of those players would be legitimate, beneficial partners to work with, and which should be avoided at all cost. Just as in the industrialized economies, managers will find some Overseas Chinese and other local companies that appear more desirable as partners than others: some Overseas Chinese companies have larger networks, greater competency in an area of the business where the foreign company is most lacking, or seem more trustworthy and upright than other partners. Previous successful working relationships with other foreign companies provide a good indication of the desirability of local companies. The multinationals' managers should use this information to move independently into a product market, or to make a decision rapidly if a desirable partner approaches with an opportunity.

As we discussed in previous chapters, Overseas Chinese companies exhibit great speed in decision-making. Unlike Japanese firms, which sometimes seem to move glacially, the Overseas Chinese network companies move quickly and expect rapid decisions from their potential partners; a multinational following standard operating procedures will probably lose several good opportunities. To move rapidly, however, managers cannot wait until they perceive a potential opportunity to research a market; they must have the knowledge substantially on hand and as Slywotzky and Shapiro (1993) say, 'leverage to beat the odds'.

To succeed in Asia, Western multinationals must develop flexible corporate cultures, which can respond to diverse managerial cultures, promote cultural sensitivity and seek out home/host similarities. The best way to manage Asian operations is with Asians. Managers must have close links in each country to speed decision-making and have ready access to the highest levels of corporate management. Using more locals with strong local connections, and building trust-based relationships, constitute some of the ways to establish stronger links to local information. However, if the multinational cannot locate suitable locals, somewhere in the multinational's management groups, someone generally exists whose background has probably better prepared them to deal with the Asian environment than is the norm for the company's managers. Philips selected a highly trusted and historically successful Mexican executive from its Latin American operations, Reinaldo Wences, to become general manager of their

---

Due diligence in Hong Kong –
or The tale of Sherlock Holmes vs. the informational void

Due diligence investigation forms a thriving industry in Hong Kong. Potential business partners are investigated to ensure that they have a sound corporate history and are likely to meet their side of any agreements and contracts. US companies constitute the biggest users of due diligence advisors, usually in relation to prospective partners in China and Hong Kong. Such external advice can prove highly valuable to foreign companies, especially those operating in China where poorly enforced business regulations may prevent the recovery of losses from fraudulent or unsatisfactory partners. One prominent accounting firm has about 300 full-time staff working in China on due diligence work alone.

---

regional headquarters in Singapore. Philips made this appointment on the premise that the Latin American environment, with its high uncertainty, poor information base, and highly personal, autocratic style of management would better prepare an executive for Asia than would working in their European headquarters; in this instance at least, the company appears to have made the right decision.

Multinationals operating in Asia should provide experience-based training programs and staff Asian operations with line managers rather than people who have come up in staff functions. Line managers can better understand their senior counterparts at most Asian firms as they will have had many of the same operational experiences. Line management experience will also help top managers to build local information links more rapidly: the senior Asian managers with which they will interact should relate to line managers more as equals than they do with staff managers.

Finally, managers should learn to recognize the evolution of Asian relationships. Unlike many other networks around the world, an individual enjoys flexible acceptance within an Overseas Chinese network. Acceptance can vary due to events over which the individual has no influence: the individual's acceptance does not depend solely on the individual's actions, but also upon others that affect situation(s) in which the individual interacts with the network. Western managers do not have total freedom to undertake some behaviors that may help cement their position with an Overseas Chinese network. (This has nothing to do with bribery, but with freedom to act independently and to involve their families in business relationships as completely as the Overseas Chinese often do.) Given this situation, Western managers must learn to recognize the cues given by the Chinese to indicate the state of a relationship between two people at any one time.

Specific implications for multinationals

Based on experiences and research with foreign operations in Asia, we now offer specific recommendations dealing with multinationals' strategic competitiveness, human resource practices, technology, contracts, distribution, promotion and pricing.

Strategic competitiveness

The strong defensive positions of the Overseas Chinese – however aggressive the Overseas Chinese may seem because of their speed of strategy formulation and market implementation, they basically employ defensive strategies. Their strategies seek to generate profits through maintaining an environment that shields two of their core competencies – their decision-making style and their control of information in an informational void. Without the informational void, Overseas Chinese companies could face severe challenges from non-network, local firms, and from foreign multinationals with competitive advantages in product and process technology, R&D, advertising and promotional skills, distribution and finances. The informational void gives the Overseas Chinese companies the ability to compete with foreign multinationals by trading their contacts for the multinationals' advantages. The informational void also reduces domestic competition for the Overseas Chinese by hindering the growth of non-network companies: these local, non-network companies would compete directly against the Overseas Chinese in the various product/markets, and would provide foreign multinationals with alternative local, Asian strategic partners.

The poor offensive positions of the Overseas Chinese – unlike Japanese firms, few of the Overseas Chinese companies appear likely to develop strong competitive positions within the foreign multinationals' home markets in the short term barring significant investments in managerial personnel. The Overseas Chinese core competency of decision-making becomes both their strength and weakness. Until Overseas Chinese companies develop a core competency less dependent on their home environments, as the large Japanese and Korean firms did, they will fail as strong competitors outside the seemingly maze-like environments serving as their bastion. This weakness implies that foreign multinationals investing in research, data acquisition and contacts, can attack Overseas Chinese competitors in their home markets: conversely, the majority of Overseas Chinese companies will have difficulty retaliating against the multinationals in their own home markets.

Human resource practices

Rotation of staff for MNCs – the core competencies of the Overseas Chinese companies (discussed in the previous chapter) also indicate that many foreign multinationals' practices of rotating executives in foreign postings every two or three years are counterproductive in fighting the competition. First, the rotations diminish the multinationals' abilities to employ emergent strategies in Asia. This effect occurs because the multinationals' managers often fall short of gaining the intimate knowledge of the market: they cannot recognize the emerging patterns in the environments or in the companies' local operations, and, consequently, cannot generate effective, Asia-based emergent strategies. Second, companies do not build contacts, humans do. When multinationals rotate employees out of Asian countries, they lose the employees' contacts. The damage may prove minimal because in the short period of two or three years, the employees could not have had opportunities to build substantial numbers of influential contacts. However, if after three years, the multinationals' managers could socialize with the local business communities effectively and build contacts, the multinationals were probably only starting to get substantial returns from those managers. One should also remember that Asians owe loyalty to individuals, and view trust as something earned between individuals. Additionally, many Asians do not perceive trust and loyalty as transferable. The incoming managers will not receive the benefits of any goodwill their predecessors built up during their time on the job. These two reasons appear especially valid when the multinationals choose to operate in Asia without local partners.

Staff's morale in the network – bright, non-family managers working for Overseas Chinese companies often wish they worked for someone else, providing opportunities for multinationals to acquire experienced local executives. Recent surveys have shown that executives of local Hong Kong companies feel out of place and dissatisfied with their employment; most would prefer to work for companies where they could contribute to corporate strategy and to aspire to top managerial positions (*The Economist*, 1996). However, many Overseas Chinese companies buy their managers' loyalties through substantial annual performance bonuses and generous retirement schemes, something some Western companies have been known to do.

Product/technology

The widespread lack of respect for intellectual property rights severely affects product management in Asia. Many attribute the problem to no rule of law: the Indian government openly uses this argument in urging multinationals to invest in India rather than in other parts of Asia. The truth appears worse in many respects.

Intellectual property rights project difficult issues when countries are striving to develop domestic manufacturing capacities. During the eighteenth and early nineteenth centuries, the fledgling US government adopted policies of acquiring foreign technology, legally or illegally, and recruiting skilled foreign craftsmen (Heilbroner and Singer, 1984). Developing countries have economic incentives to ignore intellectual property rights: the developing countries need the new technologies to move into higher value-added industries that industrialized nations control. As we indicated in an earlier chapter, in Confucian societies, this economic basis for ignoring intellectual property rights is strengthened by these rights never existing historically. With no historical precedence for intellectual property rights, protecting them becomes highly problematical. To enforce intellectual property rights, the government must shift a people's way of thinking from situations where not only the violaters feel persecuted, but the lower and middle level legal authorities probably also feel that they are unjustly persecuting the violaters. In such situations, local legal authorities will ignore property right violations when given even minimal incentives to do so.

Additionally, Confucian societies have generally not enjoyed rule of law in commercial transactions. Western-style commercial law did not evolve in Confucian cultures. The present, sorely underdeveloped, legal systems have significant weaknesses enforcing laws that have been promulgated in more recent times. Also, the Confucian cultures' ethical structure, based on the context of established relationships, affects the ethical perception of intellectual property rights. Most intellectual property pirates have no relationship with the companies or individuals from which they steal; hence, they owe no ethical duties to those companies or individuals.

Finally, with reference to China, unlike the old communist era, the present government does not rule with an iron fist throughout China. The power of the provincial governments relative to the central government has increased significantly in recent years. This power shift has increased the central government's difficulties in enforcing its laws and treaties without the provincial governments' strong support. In some instances, the provincial governments refuse to render this support. In many respects, the situation resembles the old imperial efforts to prevent the Chinese traders from conducting their overseas trading operations. Central authorities passed and tried to enforce their edicts only to be frustrated by the merchant traders and their networks of contacts among the local authorities.

Though multinationals should move production of products as close to major markets as possible, they should also consider the differences that can exist between a country's legal statutes and what can be considered the 'natural law', or the country's ethical perceptions; the latter are very powerful and difficult for mere legal statutes to overturn in the short term. So far, besides India, the major Asian country's most successful in protecting intellectual property rights are Singapore and Thailand, with Malaysia making an increasingly successful effort.

Contract flexibility

Many Western businessmen conducting business in Asia have problems with the seeming flexibility of contractual agreements. The Bundesbank's difficulties in collecting on some of their loans to Chinese companies, including government-owned firms, present a classic example. When Chinese debtor companies ceased paying on loans, Bundesbank's representatives demanded resumption of payments. Their Chinese counterparts responded by saying that circumstances had changed, and hence, the terms of the contract must change. Contractual flexibility is business according to Chinese custom.

Recall the story of how the great Chinese trader Howqua paid for the amount of quicksilver he had contracted for at the new price rather than the stated contract price after the price rose abruptly. We see the other side of the coin in Howqua's story in which Western businessmen profited from the custom. Few businessmen of the present era would follow Howqua's example and freely pay a greater price than contracted. Given Confucian and Chinese custom, however, managers should not expect Chinese businessmen to forego an effort to alter contractual terms to their benefit. Contractual flexibility took hold among Chinese businessmen because of the nature of their business. Business-to-business transactions occurred largely between long-time associates at the very least, if not actual family members. Hence, if circumstances changed abruptly in favor of one party to the transaction, and to the substantial detriment of the other party to the transaction, they would renegotiate the contract so that neither party would suffer unbearably from the changed circumstances.

Distribution

Many of the limitations of distributing goods through any developing country's infrastructure apply to Southeast Asia. Due to their early and continuing dominance of most significant distributors, wholesale and retail, in the region, the Overseas Chinese companies create the same situation in the region as the major commercial families do in Latin America. In 1996, K-Mart was forced to withdraw from Singapore after a costly attempt to break into the cut-throat, minimal-margin environment in a major Asian retailing center's mass market.

Trade formed the original business of the Overseas Chinese. Despite the number of businesses the Overseas Chinese have entered into since, they have never entirely left the business of trade. Most Overseas Chinese merchants, retailers and wholesalers, are supplied by their friends or long-established business relations. Some of the larger merchant companies are supplied by companies that are members of the same business groups and networks. This network situation gives the local merchants a tremendous competitive advantage when confronted by outside competitors. In most Asian countries, discriminatory pricing is *not* an illegal practice.

Promotion and pricing

Asian cultures affect promotion practices. Firms must seek to ensure they do not offend local custom and mores, and that they remain within the law. To one extent or another, most Asian cultures are linguistically sensitive: public signboards in foreign languages are illegal in many Asian countries. Enforcement is usually lax, however, there are periodic crackdowns (recent ones occurred in Indonesia and Vietnam). Having local agencies that can keep up with local enforcement trends and protect a multinational's interests is imperative.

Pricing is often difficult for Western firms because of the additional costs associated with international business operations, but also because, when necessary, Overseas Chinese companies are able to accept very low margins due to the family control of most Overseas Chinese companies. They are also frequently able to subsidize predatory pricing practices due to the conglomerate diversification which most of the large Overseas Chinese companies have adopted. As mentioned above discriminatory pricing is not illegal in most Asian countries.

Implications for regional governments

The Overseas Chinese managers may pare labor costs and middlemen through sourcing stocks from connections abroad; however, they generally contribute much more significantly to the countries in which they operate (Haley and Haley, 1998). The Overseas Chinese companies intensify competition within indigenous industries, often forcing prices down to benefit consumers. Bulk buying, direct importing and other traditional practices provide examples of the New Asian Emperors' global connections translating to social and commercial benefits. The Overseas Chinese also facilitate global trade. Consequently, regional governments' policies should incorporate effective understanding of the Overseas Chinese companies' economic and developmental importance.

First, for regional governments, the Overseas Chinese family companies contribute to economic viability, especially in economic crises. For example, Thailand, like most regional economies dominated by the Overseas Chinese, appears down but not out despite its 1997 financial crisis. Through traditional business practices such as keeping assets liquid, lowering borrowing and demonstrating strategic flexibility and speed, the Overseas Chinese have generally survived Thailand's 1997 financial crisis and are helping to rebuild the country's economy (Vatikiotis and Daorueng, 1998).

Second, for effective governance, regional governments often have to confront and should quell local hostility towards the Overseas

Chinese. In Indonesia, the country's visible Overseas Chinese have encountered local animosity since colonial times. But, the recent 1997 economic crisis has brought about fresh, intense waves of Overseas Chinese bashing. Indonesia's wealthiest Overseas Chinese have long had escape pods for their families and businesses such as foreign homes, foreign passports and overseas bank accounts; however, the latest tensions are forcing even the middle class to consider flight. Already the Overseas Chinese middle class have triggered an outflow from Indonesia of at least US$1 billion in capital and probably much more (Gilley *et al.*, 1998). Overseas Chinese pullouts could heighten economic distress and step up ethnic violence; however, the long-term implications appear more worrying: the Overseas Chinese departures threaten to hollow-out corporate Indonesia. 'We need Chinese businesses to attract foreign investment', said Wilson Nababan, president of the credit analysis firm CISI Raya Utama in Jakarta. 'We should be encouraging them to stay not chasing them away' (quoted in Gilley *et al.*, 1998, p. 47). More importantly, Indonesia could lose a well-educated group valued for its entrepreneurial savvy and managerial abilities. 'If they start leaving we will have a vacuum of skills', says Manggi Habir, managing director of Bahana Securities in Jakarta. 'Who is going to take their place?' (quoted in Gilley *et al.*, 1998, p. 47).

Some governments are actively trying to take advantage of the Overseas Chinese networks' capabilities. As mentioned in a previous chapter, the government of Singapore, for instance, has begun maintaining a World Wide Web page with a listing of the Overseas Chinese companies and networks operating in Singapore to facilitate potential foreign collaborators contacting Overseas Chinese companies. By doing this, the government is seeking to stimulate further foreign investment in Singapore and to increase value-added production in the Island State.

Implications for researchers

Researchers need to develop theories that reflect the business practices and styles of the Overseas Chinese. Too much of what businessmen and researchers understand about the Overseas Chinese,

Singapore's Economic Development Board – or network facilitator

The Economic Development Board (EDB) of Singapore serves as the Singapore government's main mechanism to encourage the development of Singapore's 'external wing'. The EDB was created in 1961 with the primary role of attracting foreign capital to Singapore. This role has now shifted significantly to promoting Singaporean investment abroad and to this end it has offices around the world.

The EDB does not advise Singaporean companies where to invest but assists in negotiating with foreign governments and governmental authorities. If Singaporean companies intend to invest in China, for example, the EDB can assist with negotiations with the relevant provincial governments or with the government in Beijing; but the EDB leaves dealings with the municipal governments to the companies themselves. The EDB leaves advice on where to invest to private consultants. The EDB only provides this assistance if convinced that positive benefits will flow to other Singaporean companies.

The EDB also acts as a catalyst for consortia. Singapore-based companies can approach the EDB for assistance in locating suitable partners for projects. The EDB then attempts to locate such partners, either from within Singapore or from overseas. Occasionally, the EDB identifies opportunities and then alerts suitable companies to exploit them. The EDB does not charge for its services as network facilitator.

and especially about their networks' structures, just constitutes Western interpretations of their activities – without consideration of their cultural or historical origins.

Overseas Chinese networks differ significantly from US business networks. Asian networks show much more resilience than the individual firms that make up the networks (Redding, 1996). US business networks appear relatively weak and generally represent individual firms' short-term institutional interests (Mizruchi and Schwartz, 1987). Many network theorists view networks as something that managers can manipulate for the company's sole benefit (Charan, 1991) without recognizing that networks arise and exist for all involved parties' benefits. Through an institutional perspective, the Asian economies appear network-based whereas the US economy appears firm-based. Overseas Chinese networks are normative, relational, hierarchical and substantive, just as Confucianism would require them to be. Future researchers should enquire and elaborate on these characteristics to develop useful theories of the networks that may explain both Asian and Western networking behaviors and systems, and develop best-practice behaviors for the promotion of effective co-operation between the two types of networks. If, as Fei (1992) and Hamilton (1996) argue, civilizational rather than cultural differences distinguish the East and West, the implications for international business competition have been inadequately explored.

Second, researchers should enquire more specifically into how the Overseas Chinese and their networks shape industrial structures. Many Asian developing countries' economic hierarchies arise from the networks that control so much of these economies (Haley and Haley, 1997). Consequently, in order to understand and to predict the markets' evolution and development, researchers must more fully comprehend the Overseas Chinese networks' institutional and developmental roles in these markets.

The Overseas Chinese networks: concluding remarks

We now summarize the Overseas Chinese networks' strengths and weaknesses. We have already addressed many of the points in this section in different contexts and in varying depths across the book. Yet, the Overseas Chinese networks' centrality to any consideration of competing in Southeast Asian and Chinese markets, and their centrality in Western businessmen's minds and perceptions, require at least a short, consolidated summary.

The American network of Asia –
imitation is the best form of flattery

The Overseas Chinese and Overseas Indian networks are all the rage in Asian business today. Not many have heard of their new competitor, the American Network of Asia, Pacific Northwest Advisors (PNA), a consultancy based in Seattle, Washington, USA. Modeled after the regional business networks and their intimate knowledge of regional business, PNA was founded as a true network – comprising about 20 individuals who have come together, working semi-autonomously and seeking to enhance their own agenda through co-operation with their network associates. Their brochure has the following inscribed quote from Sun Tzu's *The Art of War*: 'Those who do not know the lay of the land cannot maneuver their forces. Those who do not use local guides cannot take advantage of the ground.'

PNA's first major project has been a joint venture with the city government of Beijing to find foreign investors for the Beijing Development Area (BDA), China's newest special investment zone. BDA is a 50/50 joint venture between the city government of Beijing and PNA. PNA's success has been phenomenal, helping to find over 130 investors for the BDA. PNA's success with the BDA cued the China Association of Development Zones onto the idea that there might just be another kind of network in the world, the American network, and PNA now has a contract to find investors for all of the Association's 32 development zones.

PNA generated its success by following the Taoist mixture of traditional and contrarian advice it offers to others. As traditional advice dictates, PNA set up a joint venture to operate in China. As contrarian advice dictates, it set up shop in Beijing, outside of China's booming southern coastal region; and, from the first PNA dealt with the central authorities in Beijing. Many investors in China seek to avoid dealing with Beijing by keeping their investments below US$30 million. PNA's strategy is to face things today to avoid the risk of disaster tomorrow.

Strengths

As the Overseas Chinese network companies have grown, their people spreading all over the world, their organizational structures have remained flat, and in many ways, lean. The centers, retaining substantial control, have evolved into web-network structures. The dispersed, subsidiary units remain in many ways autonomous, but retain links to the center for support. The many layers of hierarchy found in many Western and some Japanese firms do not exist. The key managers of the subsidiary units form trusted employees. They wheel and deal and expand the companies within the constraints of the centers' vision. Western management circles classify the authority and actions of the Overseas Chinese subsidiary managers as empowerment. The best of the Overseas Chinese companies have empowered their managers for years, thus the total business networks grew rapidly.

In the web networks, the subsidiaries look to headquarters for guidance on policy, for the companies' basic directional thrust or vision and for financial support. The financial relationship approximates a venture capital company's relationship with its clients. Headquarters supports field operations, gives approval to the general plan, but seeks to avoid interfering with day-to-day operations and decision-making.

The web network companies have a paternalistic culture. Employees receive substantial bonuses when they produce good results; life-long employment constitutes the norm. If the employees are among the best, in talent, trust and uprightness, their employers usually consider them as high potential candidates for becoming partners in new businesses, often with their former employers putting up all the capital. Such benefits hinder Western multinationals from hiring away the best of the Overseas Chinese companies' employees.

Finally, speed constitutes a key advantage. Traditionally, Overseas Chinese companies have been managed by ownership. Managers as owners could move rapidly, knowing how much they could risk, and not justifying their risks to irate shareholders. Many Overseas Chinese companies are now publicly held; however, frequently, their old family ownership has the tendency to run the companies as if they were still theirs, lock, stock and barrel.

Weaknesses

The Overseas Chinese network companies exhibit substantial weaknesses. Primarily, they lack procedural controls, processes and structures. The companies' managers have within their memories a model of how the networks and their members should work. Processes and procedures, policy statements and defined structures do not exist. The corporate memories maintain no institutionalized knowledge; individuals' personal memories and unique experiences capture all the corporate knowledge. So long as no personnel disruptions occur, this is not a serious problem; however, without institutional knowledge, upon any serious disruption in key personnel, corporate performance generally falls seriously.

We catalogued paternalism as a strength in the previous section, yet it also contributes to a major weakness. Due to the cultural emphasis on seniority, some companies tend to favor senior employees over younger, but better performers. This preference for seniority can significantly hinder Overseas Chinese companies from retaining promising, ambitious young managers. The tendency to honor senior staff and managers also causes problems for many companies that are trying to professionalize. The unwillingness to run counter to traditional values and seniority, manifested among many members of the Overseas Chinese companies' senior and middle managers, can cause significant tension and conflict during the professionalization process.

Their lack of proprietary capabilities poses immense problems for Overseas Chinese companies. Many Overseas Chinese companies simply do not perceive brand equity or home-grown technology as having any true value. Many of their managers believe in buying or copying technology, or if necessary, licensing products. The Southeast and East Asian economies, in which most of the Overseas Chinese companies maintain their operations, have leapfrogged from centuries of primarily village-oriented subsistence economies to decades of fantastic growth where virtually anything produced could be sold profitably. Consequently, the dominant companies have not truly accepted the concepts of marketing or product development and brand equity.

Speculations about the future

When Nakamura (1992) stated that the strategic management processes of East and Southeast Asia's newly industrializing countries were following the same pattern as Japan's had, he was arguing that the future of Asian business approximated Japan's history. This understanding is fallacious. For various reasons, some that we mentioned in earlier chapters, the future of the Overseas Chinese and their business structures and strategies in Southeast and East Asia appear likely to follow an independent course, and will interact with Western practices and behaviors in their own unique way. Managers and policy makers must determine the independent course's direction because of the market's size, and also because of potential influences on business practices globally.

Many believe that the reforms that the Asian governments are undertaking today will make the Asian economies resemble the American (Kristof, 1998). This belief follows the theory that the regulatory environments will shape business structures and competitive practice. We can also speculate on future directions by considering present-day events and trends: for example, many of the Overseas Chinese companies' heirs hold positions of authority within their family companies. What roles do they play? How do they see their futures evolving? We can classify some of the founders of today's empires, such as 53-year-old Stan Shih of Acer, as second generation. These second-generation managers have perceptions of their roles in their companies and their societies, and were willing to share their perceptions with us for this book.

The first generation of Overseas Chinese business founders took what they best could use of Confucian philosophy and discarded what they found less desirable or useful. In an earlier chapter, we noted the lack of primogeniture in Chinese culture which has significantly deterred the creation and maintenance of capital among Chinese families over the centuries. This first generation of the New Asian Emperors has largely sloughed off that burden on their fortunes. They are restructuring, reorganizing and expanding their best-run companies to where they can compete globally. Li Kai Shang has consolidated his diversified far-flung empire into a more focused business empire. At Wuthelam Group, the founder, Goh Cheng Liang, brought his son, Goh Hup Jin, back into the family business. At first flush this practice may seem like business as usual; however, Hup Jin had earned an MBA in the United States and worked in major US companies. When he returned home, his duties included helping to professionalize the company's management structure to take the company public. Goh Hup Jin, and a cadre of professionals whom he brought into the business, have professionalized management without excessively disrupting operations. To facilitate the transition, the company founded a subsidiary where skilled managers of the old school who could not adjust to the professionalization of management procedures and structures could move. These business practices exemplify the Confucian emphasis on personal loyalty, but also indicate good management.

We asked Goh Hup Jin what he felt made the management of the Overseas Chinese unique; he answered that Overseas Chinese business practices did not differ from Western practices strategically, but rather only operationally. From his vantage point, he saw no changes in the future which would affect anything of true importance in the Overseas Chinese strategy of business; changes would primarily come in controlling and reporting processes due to the continued growth of the companies.

We also discussed future changes in strategic processes with Wee Cho Yaw, chairman of United Overseas Bank, and his son and heir, Wee Ee Cheong. As they described their strategic decision-making styles, little difference emerged between the two. For example, Wee Ee Cheong told us, 'I don't let figures influence my decision...They are used to confirm the decision rather than to arrive at the decision'. Similarly, Wee Cho Yaw indicated to us, 'How a good businessman reads the ups and downs of a market is often more valuable than statistics'. Both generations of managers felt that professional mangers seemed too timid in their decision-making and tended to make too many unwarranted assumptions about the markets.

In many instances, when we spoke with both senior traditional managers and their younger more-educated heirs, we noticed remarkable similarities in their viewpoints and perspectives. The results of our interviews, research, work and yes, socializing with the New Asian Emperors, indicated that lower- and middle-level managers in Overseas Chinese companies appear to be professionalizing; yet, top-level managers continue to strategize and to manage largely drawing upon their intimate knowledge of their businesses, their people, and their markets. The strategic style will continue to focus and senior managers' draw on their judgment and character, and not the numbers. Overseas Chinese management seems to be moving towards a combination of Western management procedures and processes at lower and middle levels of management; and continues to rely on the traditional Overseas Chinese management practices in higher levels of management. Our conclusions have also been corroborated by Chan and Chiang (1994).

Indeed, some of the New Asian Emperors appear to take their superstitions as seriously as their numbers. Li Kai Shang's watch runs exactly eight minutes fast, because *baat*, the Cantonese word for eight forms a homonym for *faat*, the Cantonese word for wealth. On the roof of the nondescript China Building in Central Hong Kong from where Li runs his empire, two eighteenth-century cannons point to the recently built Entertainment Building across the street from his office. These cannons serve to deflect the bad *Feng Shui* elements emanating from the new block. We should also not forget one of the second-generation's mangers, Manuel V. Pangilinan, of Hong Kong's First Pacific Group. In 1995, when First Pacific was preparing for what eventually became a US$1.6 billion bid for commercial property in Manila, he altered the original bid after his company's geomancer indicated that the bid did not constitute a propitious figure. 'I did not want to tempt fate', Manuel Pangilinan argued; he raised his bid, unnecessarily as circumstances later revealed (*Business Week*, 2 September, 1996). Pangilinan outbid his closest competitor by some US$400 million; he would have won the bid even with his lower, unpropitious figure.

Bibliography

Blackman, C. (1997), *Negotiating China: Case Studies and Strategies*, St. Leonards, NSW, Australia: Allen & Unwin.

Chan, K. B. and C. Chiang (1994), *Stepping Out, The Making of Chinese Entrepreneurs*, Singapore: Prentice Hall.

Chan, W. T. (1963), *Chinese Philosophy*, Princeton, NJ: Princeton University Press.

Charan, R. (1991), 'How networks reshape organizations – for results,' *Harvard Business Review*, Reprint No. 91503.

Cheng, A. T. and H. Vriens (1996/97), 'Superman vs China', *Asia, Inc.*, 5(2), 42–9.

Chu, C. N. (1995), *The Asian Mind Game*, St Ives, NSW, Australia: Stealth Productions.

Chu, T. C. and T. MacMurray, (1993), 'The road ahead for Asia's leading conglomerates', *McKinsey Quarterly*, 3, 117–26.

Clegg, S. R. and G. Redding (eds) (1990), *Capitalism in Contrasting Cultures*, New York: de Gruyter.

East Asia Analytical Unit (1995), *Overseas Chinese Business Networks*, Canberra, Australia: AGPS Press, Department of Foreign Affairs and Trade.

Fei, X. (1992), *From the Soil: The Foundation of Chinese Society*, Berkeley: University of California Press.

Fernandez-Armesto, F. (1995), *Millennium*, London: Bantam Press.

Fukuyama, F. (1995), *Trust: The Social Virtues and the Creation of Prosperity*, London: Penguin Books.

Ghosh, B. C. and C. O. Chan (1994), 'A study of strategic planning behavior among emergent businesses in Singapore and Malaysia', *International Journal of Management*, **11**(2), 697–706.

Gilley, B., J. McBeth, B. Dolven and S. Tripathi (1998), 'Ready, set...', *Far Eastern Economic Review*, 19 February, 46–50.

Haley, G. T. (1997a), 'A strategic perspective on Overseas Chinese networks' decision-making', *Management Decision*, **35**(8), 587–94.

Haley, G. T. (1997b), 'The values Asia needs', *Business Times (Singapore)*, Editorial and Opinion Section, 24 December, p. 6.

Haley, G. T. and U. C. V. Haley (1997), 'Making strategic business decisions in South and Southeast Asia', *Conference Proceedings of the First International Conference on Operations and Quantitative Management*, Jaipur, India, Volume II, pp. 597–604.

Haley, G. T. and U. C. V. Haley (forthcoming, 1998), 'Boxing with shadows: competing effectively with the Overseas Chinese and Overseas Indian networks in the Asian arena', *Journal of Organizational Change Management*, **11**(4).

Haley, G. T. and C. T. Tan (1996), 'The black hole of Southeast Asia: strategic decision-making in an informational void', *Management Decision*, Special Issue on Strategic Management in the Asian Pacific, **34**(9), 43–55.

Haley, G. T. and C. T. Tan (forthcoming, 1998), 'East versus West: strategic marketing management meets the Asian networks', *Journal of Business & Industrial Marketing*, Special Issue on 'Business-to-Business Marketing in Asia', **14**(2).

Haley, U. C. V. (1997), 'The Myers-Briggs type indicator and decision-making styles: identifying and managing cognitive trails in strategic decision making', in C. Fitzgerald and L. Kirby (eds), *Developing Leaders: Research and Applications in Psychological Type and Leadership Development*, Palo Alto, CA: Consulting Psychologists Press, pp. 187–223.

Haley, U. C. V., L. Low and M. H. Toh (1996), 'Singapore incorporated: reinterpreting Singapore's business environments through a corporate metaphor', *Management Decision*, **34**(9), Special Issue on 'Strategic Management in the Asia Pacific,' pp. 21–33.

Haley, U. C. V. and S. A. Stumpf (1989), 'Cognitive trails in strategic decision-making: linking theories of personalities and cognitions', *Journal of Management Studies*, **26**(5), 477–97.

Hall, J. W. and J. G. Kirk (eds) (1988), *History of the World*, Greenwich, CT, USA: Bison Books.

Hamilton, G. G. (1996), 'The theoretical significance of Asian business networks', in G. G. Hamilton (ed.), *Asian Business Networks*, Berlin, New York: Walter de Gruyter, pp. 283–298.

Heilbroner, R. L. and A. Singer (1984), *The Economic Transformation of America: 1600 to the Present*, 2nd edition, New York: Harcourt Brace Jovanovich Publishers.

Hiscock, G. (1997), *Asia's Wealth Club*, London: Allen Unwin.

Hofer, C. W. and D. Schendel (1978), *Strategy Formulation: Analytical Concepts*, St. Paul, MN: West Publishing Co.

Hofstede, G. (1994), 'Cultural constraints in management theories', *International Review of Strategic Management*, Vol. 5, D. E. Hussey (ed.), West Sussex, UK: John Wiley & Sons, Ltd, pp. 27–47.

Hsu, P. S. C. (1984), 'The comparison of family structure and values on business organizations in Oriental cultures, a comparison of China and Japan', *Proceedings of the 1984 AMA Conference, Singapore*, pp. 754–68.

Khanna, T. and K. Palepu (1997), 'Why focused strategies may be wrong for emerging markets', *Harvard Business Review*, July/August.

Kohut, J., and A. T. Cheng (1996), 'Return of the merchant mandarins', *Asia, Inc.*, March, pp. 22–31.

Kotkin, J. (1994), *Tribes: How Race, Religion and Identity Determine Success in the New Global Economy*, New York: Random House.

Kristoff, N. D. (1998), 'Crisis pushing Asian capitalism closer to US-style free market,' *New York Times* (internet edition) Jan. 17.

Lau, D. C. (1963), *Lao Tzu: Tao Te Ching*, London: Penguin Books.

Lau, D. C. (1995), *Mencius Says*, Singapore: Federal Publications, Pte Ltd.

Legge, J. (1970), *The Works of Mencius*, New York: Cover Publications, Inc.

Mintzberg, H. (1987), 'Crafting strategy', *Harvard Business Review*, July/August, pp. 66–75.

Mintzberg, H. (1994), 'The fall and rise of strategic planning', *Harvard Business Review*, January/February, pp. 107–114.

Mintzberg, H. and J. Waters (1985), 'Of strategies, deliberate and emergent', *Harvard Business Review*, 6, pp. 257–272.

Mizruchi, M. S. and M. Schwartz (1987), *Intercorporate Relations: The Structural Analysis of Business*, Cambridge, UK: Cambridge University Press.

Nakamura, G. I. (1992), 'Development of strategic management in the Asia Pacific region', in D. E. Hussey (ed.), *International Review of*

Strategic Management, volume 3, West Sussex: John Wiley & Sons, pp. 3–18.

Nohria, N. and R. G. Eccles (1992), *Networks and Organizations: Structure, Form and Action*, Cambridge, MA: Harvard Business School Press.

Pan, C. C. H. (1984), 'Confucian philosophy: implication to management', *Proceedings of the 1984 AMA Conference, Singapore*, pp. 777–81.

Prahalad, C. K. and G. Hamel (1990), 'The core competence of the corporation', *Harvard Business Review*, May/June, pp. 79–91.

Putti, J. M. (1991), *Management: Asia Context*, Singapore: McGraw-Hill.

Radelet, S. and J. Sachs (1997), 'Asia's re-emergence', *Foreign Affairs*, November/December, pp. 44–59.

Redding, S. G. (1986), 'Entrepreneurship in Asia', *Euro-Asia Business Review*, **5**(4), 23–7.

Redding, S. G. (1993), *The Spirit of Chinese Capitalism*, New York: de Gruyter.

Redding, S. G. (1995), 'Overseas Chinese networks: understanding the enigma,' *Long Range Planning*, **28**(1), 61–9.

Redding, S. G. (1996), 'Weak organization and strong linkages: managerial ideology and Chinese family business networks', in G. G. Hamilton (ed.), *Asian Business Networks*, Berlin, New York: Walter de Gruyter, pp. 27–42.

Rohwer, J. (1995), *Asia Rising*, Singapore: Butterworth-Heinemann, Asia.

Seagrave, S. (1996), *Lords of the Rim*, London: Bantam Press.

Shigematsu, S. (1994), 'The study of Overseas South Asians: retrospect and prospect,' Working Paper, Graduate School of International Development, Nagoya University, Japan.

Slywotsky, A. J. and B. P. Shapiro (1993), 'Leveraging to beat the odds: the new marketing mind-set', *Harvard Business Review*, September/October, pp. 97–107.

Tan S. U. (1991), *Letters from Thailand*, Bangkok, Thailand: Editions Duang Kamol.

The Economist (1996), 'The limits of family values', in a special 'Survey of Business in Asia,' 9–15 March, pp. 12–22.

Vatikiotis, M. (1998), 'The Chinese Way', *Far Eastern Economic Review*, 26 February, p. 45.

Vatikiotis, M. and P. Daorueng (1998), 'Survival tactics', *Far Eastern Economic Review*, 26 February, 42–45.

Wada, K. (1992), *Yaohan's Global Strategy, the 21st Century is the Era of Asia*, Hong Kong: Capital Communications Corporation, Ltd.

Waley, A. (1996), *Confucius: The Analects*, Ware, Hertfordshire, UK: Wordsworth Editions, Ltd.

Wang, G. (1991), *China and the Chinese Overseas*, Singapore: Times Academic Press.

Weidenbaum, M. and S. Hughes (1996), *Bamboo Network*, New York: Martin Kessler Books.

Yamashita, S. (1991), 'Japan's Role as a Regional Technological Integrator in the Pacific Rim', paper presented at the Conference on the Emerging Technological Trajectory of the Pacific Rim, Tufts University, Medford, MA, 4–6 October.

Yong, C. F. (1987), *A Short Biography of Tan Kah Kee*, Singapore: Tan Kah Kee Foundation.

In addition to the above, countless articles in the following publications have provided background and depth:

Asia, Inc.
Asia Pacific Economic Review
AsiaWeek
Asian Business
Business Times (of Singapore)
Business Week
Far Eastern Economic Review
Forbes
Fortune
International Herald Tribune
Los Angeles Times
New York Times
Next (of Hong Kong)
The Australian
The Economist
The Straits Times (of Singapore)
Time Magazine

Appendix A: Topic Category Names for Chapter 4 Tables

Topic	Full topic name
Marketing	Marketing
Pricing	Pricing
Promotion	Promotion
Distrib	Distribution
Prod dev	Product development
Channels	Channels of distribution
Buyer beh	Buyer behavior
Cons beh	Consumer behavior
Demograph	Demographics
Advert	Advertising
Prod mgt	Product management
Sales mgt	Sales management
In-store	In-store promotion
Bus res	Business research
Mgt res	Management research
Mkt res	Marketing research
Cons res	Consumer research
Ind mkt	Industrial marketing
Tran/log	Transportation or logistics
Strat mgt	Strategic management
Mgt decis	Management decision
Culture	Culture
Media hab	Media habits
Mass comm	Mass communications
Strat plan	Strategic planning

Index

ABI-Inform database, 75
Academic publications:
  Southeast Asia, 75–87
Acer Computers, 24, 49,
  90–1, 94–5
Apple, 15
Asia Brewery, 24
Asia Pacific Breweries, 24
Authoritarianism, 37, 64
  decision-making, 103
Aw Kim Chen, 117
Batavia:
  massacre of Overseas
    Chinese, 57
Benefits:
  Japanese and Chinese
    expectations compared,
    68–9
Bonuses, 151
Brand names, 90–1, 136–7
Breaches of faith, 17
The Buddha, 30, 34–5
Buddhism, 29, 31–2
  ethical behavior, 43
Business culture:
  Japanese and Overseas
    Chinese compared,
    64–9
Business education:
  Overseas Chinese, 57, 92,
    113
Business publications:
  closely held information,
    133
  Southeast Asia, 75–87
Cambodia:
  Overseas Chinese, 9–10
Chan, C.O., 125, 136
Chan, W.T., 117, 155
Charan, Ram, 14–16, 18, 149
Charitable activities, 23
Charoen Pokhphand (CP
  Group), 99–100, 122,
  124–5
Chearavanont, Dhanin, 124
Chearavanont family, 100,
  122
Cheng, A.T., 120
Cheng Ho, 11
Chiang, C., 117, 155

China:
  and the Overseas Chinese,
    135
  intellectual property
    rights, 143–4
Chu, T.C., 66, 95, 99, 121
Clans, 13–15
Coke, 137
Colonialist influences, 62,
  64, 80
Competitive advantage, 14,
  16, 96
  control of information,
    131–2
  guanxi, 132–3
  Overseas Chinese, 130–3
  speed in decision-making,
    130–1, 151
Competitive disadvantages:
  blind-siding, 136
  family limits, 137–8
  home turf only, 134
  Overseas Chinese, 133–8
  poor proprietary
    capabilities, 136–7, 152
Confucianism, 23, 28–49
  ethical behavior, 43, 45–6
  influence on Overseas
    Chinese trade and
    economics, 36–41
Confucius, 28–34, 39
Contract flexibility, 144–5
Coolies, 6, 56
Core competency, 108–9
  control of information,
    121–2, 131–2
  decision-making style,
    121–2
  networks, 123, 132–3
  Overseas Chinese, 120–5
  speed in decision-making,
    121, 130–1, 151
Creative Technology, 24, 90,
  134
Criminal networks, 21
Culture, 6, 57
  differences, 97
Daimler Benz, 24
Dao Heng Bank, 24
Daorueng, P., 146

Decision-making, 95–103
  action-driven, 102–3
  hands-on experience, 98–9
  holistic information
    processing, 102
  qualitative information,
    100–1
  speed, 121, 130–1, 151
  transfer of knowledge,
    99–100
Discontinuities, 109, 114–15
Distribution, 22, 145
Diversification, 62, 63, 64,
  92, 99–100, 120, 122
Due diligence investigation,
  139
Duty, 40, 43
Economic influence of
  Overseas Chinese,
  12–13
Education:
  Overseas Chinese, 57, 92,
    113
Embarassment, 15
Empowerment, 151
Ethical behavior, 43, 45–6,
  48–9, 54
  Japanese and Chinese
    culture compared, 67–8
Exports:
  Southeast Asia, 74
'Face', 15
  losing, 16
Family, 13–15, 38, 40, 42–3
  Indonesian conglomerates,
    60
  Overseas Chinese
    business networks, 58–9
Family businesses:
  Overseas Chinese, 90,
    92–6
Family limits:
  competitive disadvantage,
    137–8
Fathers, 38, 40, 42–3
Federal Flour Mills Bhd,
  123
Federation of Hokkien
  Associations of
  Malaysia, 53

Inde